2

Withdrawn

11/09

GRASPING THE RING II

Nine People Who Matter

By Gene A. Budig

Foreword by
Thomas Curley

Published by
The News-Gazette, Inc.

The News-Gazette®

EDITOR AND PUBLISHER   John Foreman
PROJECT EDITOR   Amy George
ART DIRECTOR   Joan Millis

Cover design and book layout: Joan Millis, The News-Gazette

Hard cover ISBN: 978-0-9798420-6-1

Printed in the United States of America

The News-Gazette, Inc.
15 Main Street
Champaign, IL 61820
Phone: (217) 351-5252
Fax: (217) 351-5245
www.news-gazette.com

For the Next Generation:
Regan, Jack, Nicholas, and A.J.

And for those of this era who advised and edited:
Dixie Clark, Kay Gallagher, Alan Heaps, Rich Levin,
Robin O'Callaghan, Andrew Schwartz,
Nancy Viggiano, Don Walton, and Dick Marshall.

Proceeds from the sale of this book that are due the
author will go to the College Board's National
Commission on Writing, a group of leaders from
education, business, and industry who see the
immediate need for increased strength
in such an essential area.

CONTENTS

FOREWORD
by Thomas Curley

*In a series of well chosen words, highly descripitive para-
graphs, and compelling content, Professor Gene A. Budig tells
the personalized stories of nine exceptional Americans—people who knew what they wanted in life and followed difficult
paths to achieve their admirable ends.*

*What becomes apparent to the reader is that these individ-
uals were ahead of their time, and the essays paint a vivid and
sometimes troubling picture of what they endured to become
leaders of stature.*

*Budig knows the selected nine and picked them with care,
as the content attests, and he conversed with them and informed associates and family members about the details for
the book. Without a doubt, each of them has grasped the ring
of national achievement and set high goals for those who will
follow.*

*Each has experienced numerous highs and lows in his or
her quest, and that is precisely what* Grasping the Ring II *is all
about. It is about courage, will, and challenge. As a group, they
are characterized by situations that demanded insight and
luck, and now they appear as heroes and trendsetters in the
public eye.*

*One cannot forget the often-dangerous road that Rachel
and Jackie Robinson chose to travel. He was a Hall of Fame
baseball player for the Brooklyn Dodgers and the first African
American to crash the color barrier of Major League Baseball.
She was the principled and steel-willed mate behind his hero-
ics. Rachel and Jackie started the long and often bitter march
for equal rights as a team, a decade before the arrival of Dr.
Martin Luther King, Jr. They encountered numerous threats,
and they were always draining and ugly.*

Showman Bill Veeck taught baseball fans how to laugh and

cry during his successful ownership runs in Cleveland, Chicago, and St. Louis. With considerable fanfare and criticism, he signed Larry Doby to a contract with the Indians, making him the African American ever to play in the American League. This decision led Cleveland to an AL pennant and a World Series Championship in 1948, and Doby to a place of honor in the Hall of Fame. To the amusement of many baseball fans and to the consternation of his fellow owners, Veeck hired Eddie Gaedel, who stood three-foot, seven-inches, to pinch-hit for the Browns. The League immediately stepped in and ended the laughter and the one-day career of Gaedel.

Sports fans immediately recognize Bob Costas on the streets of New York, because many of them grew up watching his acclaimed work on NBC Sports. Since his burst on the national scene in 1979, he has covered every major sport, but is perhaps most identified with the Olympics and baseball. He has anchored NBC's primetime coverage of the last five summer Olympics and is scheduled to host coverage of the 2012 summer games in London. His book, Fair Ball, a Fan's Case for Baseball, *was a bestseller. A native of Queens, New York, he attended Syracuse University and studied communications. Costas has won 19 Emmy Awards and been chosen National Sportscaster of the Year an unprecedented eight times.*

Countless Americans knew Gene Autry as the Singing Cowboy, long-time star of radio, recordings, movies, and television. He was so popular that he, at times, drew more movie fans than his friend, John Wayne. Autry never finished high school and later in life became a zealous advocate of education at all levels. At his death on October 2, 1998, he had given charities in the Los Angeles area more than $250 million, always without notice. His estate still gives, and it is interesting to note that Autry has given more than the late Paul Newman, a popular movie star, known and respected for his generosity. Always a *baseball fan, Autry was persuaded to purchase the Los Angeles Angels in 1961 and he later moved the club to nearby Anaheim where they became the California Angels. The purchase gave him many hours of enjoyment because he always kept a scorecard.*

As a youngster growing up in the ghetto of Omaha, Bob Gibson was not sure of his favorite sport. Clearly, it was between basketball and baseball. Bob was 15 years old when his American Legion baseball team became the Nebraska state champion. He went on to play basketball on a full scholarship at Creighton University, a Jesuit school in Omaha near his home. He was so good he later became the first member of the Creighton Sports Hall of Fame, largely for his basketball achievements. He settled, however, on a career in baseball, signing with the St. Louis Cardinals of the National League and going on to win 251 games, losing 174, posting an extraordinary 2.91 earned run average, and striking out 3,117 batters. Remembering the first time he saw Gibson pitch, Joe Torre, manager of the Los Angeles Dodgers, said that "when necessary he had three pitches … fast, faster, and fastest." He also said he would not describe Gibson as unfriendly when he pitched, "hateful was more like it." Gibson played in St. Louis from 1959 to 1975.

Perhaps the most recognizable sports figure on the Bay Area sports scene, Oakland Athletics vice president and general manager Billy Beane is well known for fielding successful baseball teams with financial constraints. For example, in 2006, the A's ranked 21st of 30 Major League Baseball teams in player salaries, but had the 5th-best regular season record. That reflected a typical season for the personable man who sometimes wears shorts and sandals to work at the Coliseum. His unorthodox operational genius was the essence of Michael Lewis's Moneyball, *the hugely influential 2003 book that changed the thinking of many in baseball, and especially the owners who wanted to learn how to win more and pay less. The book that riled his colleagues at the operational levels of other clubs, the so-called establishment of MLB, is soon to become a feature length movie.*

Jerry West grew up in the hills of West Virginia and learned to play basketball on a dirt-covered court with a bent hoop nailed to a storage shed. As a youngster, he would practice in wind, rain, and even snow until his hands bled. He often skipped meals in favor of more practice time. West went on to be an All-State high school player, drawing the interest of more than 60 universities. The shy youngster decided to go where he would feel at home, West Virginia University at Morgantown. He became a consensus All-American as a forward, taking the Mountaineers to the final game of the NCAA Tournament in 1958, and losing 71-70 to the University of California at Berkeley, West was named the Most Outstanding Player of the national tourney. Along with Oscar Robertson, he co-captained the U.S. men's basketball team at the 1960 summer Olympics that won the gold medal. His 14 years with Los Angeles resulted in 14 NBA All-Star games and a long string of victories for the Lakers. He was arguably professional basketball's finest guard at both ends of the court.

One of the most interesting personalities in professional sports is Stan Kasten, the only person to hold the position of president of three different teams simultaneously. Another claim to fame for Kasten was that he learned his trade working along side entrepreneur Ted Turner, the often contentious and unpredictable owner of the three franchises in Atlanta. Kasten survived and prospered with Turner for a quarter of a century. "No two days were alike with Ted," Kasten recalled. "He left productive people pretty much alone." The Turner-Kasten tandem brought the city of Atlanta numerous wins with the Braves, the Hawks, and the Thrashers. During the

Kasten presidency, the Atlanta Braves won more games than any other team in Major League Baseball. Turner sold his teams in 2001. With an imposing resume and three years on the sidelines, Kasten surfaced as president of the expansion Washington Nationals and directed the planning and building of a new ballpark, like he did in Atlanta.

Professor Budig worked with Commissioner Bud Selig on a regular basis for more than six years as president of Major League Baseball's American League. He knew Selig well early in his tenure as commissioner—what he was like and what he was about. He saw his values and mode of operation up close. Despite reports to the contrary, Selig was always complex and difficult for some of his colleagues to understand, Budig said. Detailing the highs and lows of being the person in charge of Major League Baseball, Budig takes pains to offer a unique view of the unrelenting criticism that accompanies the office of commissioner and the often-overlooked record of long-term accomplishment. He provides us with a telling picture of Selig, who gave a revealing set of observations in a recent speech to a couple of thousand teachers in Houston.

In Grasping the Ring, *released in 2008, Budig authored interpretive essays on acquaintances like New York Yankees owner George M. Steinbrenner, Hall of Fame outfielder Larry Doby, Nebraska football coach Tom Osborne, North Carolina basketball coach Roy Williams, famed running back Gale Sayers, Chicago White Sox and Bulls owner Jerry Reinsdorf, Medal of Honor winner Bob Kerrey, pioneering journalist Al Neuharth, and former U.S. Senator and presidential nominee Bob Dole.*

According to Bob Costas, who wrote the foreward for the first Grasping the Ring, *Dr. Budig has had a long and remarkable career himself, serving as the president/chancellor at three major state universities (Illinois State University, West Virginia University, and the University of Kansas), as past*

president of Major League Baseball's American League, and
as a professor at five universities, including the University of
Nebraska-Lincoln and Princeton University.
He is a retired major general in the Air
National Guard/United States Air Force.

AP Photo

  "Despite these impressive achievements,
I have always found Gene to be unassuming
and self-effacing. It is typical of him to be so
genuinely interested in the stories and per-
spectives of others," Costas wrote.

Thomas Curley
President of the Associated Press

INTRODUCTION

With the release of *Grasping the Ring* in 2008, more than a few of my associates and critics from the worlds of higher education and sports grumbled about who was not included in the book. They applauded the nine individuals who were selected and featured, but said the number was simply too small and clearly unrealistic. They were correct, of course. But the most vociferous criticism came from those whose nominees did not make the final cut for inclusion in the book.

Several months after the release of the book of biographical essays on prominent public figures, significant sales, and an encouraging number of positive reviews, I decided to go back to the word processor and produce *Grasping the Ring II.*

I have been most fortunate to meet, converse with, and introduce many interesting people, some of whom have been seen on the front pages of America's newspapers and on evening news telecasts over the past four decades.

Presidents of the United States, senators and representatives, governors, members of the Supreme Court, and international dignitaries have passed my way because of the exceptional institutions that I have been fortunate enough to represent.

Other notable visitors to the University of Nebraska-Lincoln, Illinois State University, West Virginia University, the University of Kansas, and the 30 ballparks of Major League Baseball have included high-profile titans from business and industry, college and university presidents, labor leaders, journalists, Nobel laureates, Pulitzer Prize winners, distinguished professors, and outstanding teachers, and stage, television, and movie personalities, among others.

Most of them have had timely and challenging substance to offer, especially to eager, impressionable young college students.

And varied experience from elders, with graying or no hair, has its value especially in this ever-changing, economically-challenged, and uncertain world.

Among the long parade of intriguing people, I have singled out only 18 of them; each was compelling, but in a different way. No two were alike. Each had unshakable values, some of which were hard to understand and appreciate at the time, and each dared to confront overwhelming odds to make a real difference and, though not always the case, to gain a unique place in American history.

Each was, at times, complex and private and each delivered a measure of hope and strength. Some were humble, others were not. Some were more likable than others, and some were outrageous by any accepted norm. Admittedly, many more people could have been singled out; no slight is intended.

The selectees for *Grasping the Ring II* are Rachel Robinson, Bill Veeck, Bob Costas, Gene Autry, Bob Gibson, Billy Beane, Jerry West, Stan Kasten, and Allan H. "Bud" Selig, commissioner of Major League Baseball. Those appearing in volume one were George M. Steinbrenner, Larry Doby, Tom Osborne, Roy Williams, Gale Sayers, Jerry Reinsdorf, Bob Kerrey, Al Neuharth, and Bob Dole.

Uniquely, these individuals are linked by their differences. They sometimes bear little resemblance to one another in terms of their personal characteristics, and yet they share certain values and traits that engender public notice, interest, respect, and downright irritation. Those selected have enormous strengths and some very visible shortcomings. They are, after all, human.

For the record, I have known each of the 18 for a considerable length of time, and each was responsive to my sometimes difficult questions and other times naïve inquires. Some were, I must confess, more patient than others. They rightfully questioned a few of my conclusions, as I thought they would. Each has added to my understanding, and it was especially meaningful to me that each recalled a specific issue in which I had played a significant role.

The people featured in the two books did not seek attention; in truth, they did me and the readers a favor. They certainly widened my horizons on a number of pressing and timeless issues and on ways to experience inner satisfaction. They were candid at all times.

More than 100 people helped me gather information on these 18 subjects, and offered thoughtful and spirited interpretations of the findings. They liked to debate the contributions of the 18 and often they disagreed, but their contributions were essential. Fairness and objectivity were paramount throughout the data gathering process, which took three years. Those who gave a hand included newspaper reporters and columnists, media notables, politicians, college football and basketball coaches, past and current baseball players, managers and owners, academics, publishers, family members and friends of the 18 selected, and more than a few critics.

Importantly, all evoked heartfelt emotions regardless of differing takes on matters large and small.

Gene A. Budig

A Special Time . . .

Jackie Robinson is inducted into the Baseball Hall of Fame
at Cooperstown, New York, with his wife Rachel and Branch Rickey,
general manager of the Dodgers, sharing the moment.

A
national treasure,
Rachel Robinson

At a gala dinner honoring music industry giant Clive Davis, famed educator Johnnetta Cole, and film legend George Lucas in New York, I was reminded that Rachel Robinson exemplifies so much of what Americans today hold dear.

Without question, she embodies the values of her late husband, Jackie Robinson, the first African American to play baseball in the major leagues as a member of the old Brooklyn Dodgers. She knew and loved baseball, and she rarely missed one of Jackie's home games at historic Ebbets Field.

Rachel Robinson knows what she and Jackie represented both on and off the field. They preceded Dr. Martin Luther King, Jr., by more than a decade on the civil rights scene, always espousing what they believed was right and proper with regard to human rights and dignity.

"They were a highly visible team of courageous people," said Len Coleman, the former president of Major League Baseball's National League, the league where Jackie made his name as a Hall of Fame player. Coleman was, like Jackie, a superior athlete, the first African American to score a touchdown for Princeton University.

Rachel Robinson has tirelessly carried forth the message of Jackie Robinson—one of fairness, racial equity, and opportunity for all people—with enormous grace and effectiveness. Through the Jackie Robinson Foundation, and with the love and active support of many, she has built one of the nation's foremost organizations for assisting able young minority students.

More than 1,200 young scholars have been identified and

funded for their college experience by the foundation, which
Coleman, its chairman, calls "a symbol of hope for a united
American society." He, Rachel, and the Robinsons' daughter,
Sharon, have spearheaded, with far-reaching success, the effort
to obtain funds needed for the foundation's growth and develop-
ment.

They once asked me, as former president of the American
League, to join them in acquiring needed resources from the
Yawkey Trust, since Mr. and Mrs. Tom Yawkey owned the Boston
Red Sox for many years during the time of Ted Williams, who
admired Robinson as a player and as a man.

Former Red Sox chairman, John Harrington, a confidant of
the Yawkeys, has nothing but fond memories of Jackie Robinson
as a gifted player and as an inspired activist, someone who fear-
lessly pushed for needed societal change.

Harrington was especially complimentary of Rachel, whom
he believes has continued the Robinson message of "hope and
change for generations." She deserves, he thinks, her own place
in American history. With his active encouragement, the Yawkey
Trust gave the Robinson Foundation more than three million dollars, one of its largest gifts. He also attended the annual Robinson
Foundation dinner in New York.

There was a time, not too many years ago, when many people
thought the message of Jackie and Rachel Robinson was some-
how divisive, something to be feared, and something to be opposed. There were numerous death threats against Jackie Robinson during his ten-year playing career in Brooklyn.

With enormous inner resolve and strength, this woman of
conviction has carried the message of her often-embattled husband and the often-contentious Civil Rights Movement to all corners of the United States and around the globe. "One cannot say
enough about her contributions to people everywhere," Commissioner Bud Selig has said on numerous occasions. Reggie Jackson,

an outspoken African American great of the game, has referred to her as "an angel of hope."

Without question, Rachel Robinson has been many things to many people and no single description does her justice. She has been a civil rights activist, social pioneer, professor, nurse, wife, and mother. She is driven by the belief that education is the way out for many youngsters in our society, and she further believes that no life should be wasted because of denied educational opportunity.

One of Jackie Robinson's friends and teammates on the Dodgers, Joe Black, once reminded Len Coleman and me at a World Series game that Jackie had "the power to lead as a player and a person" and that Rachel had the "will and grit" to carry important ideas to fruition. "They were the perfect team," he thought. Black also often said, "All of us had to wait for Jackie."

Buck O'Neil was a batting champion and a highly successful manager in the old Negro American League who sent the likes of Ernie Banks, Satchel Page, and Elston Howard to the major leagues. O'Neil remembered Rachel as "tough and tender at the same time," and he especially admired her spirit, an "eternal gift."

Rachel can be direct in a respectful and humorous way. When I asked her about the historic election of President Obama and how Jackie would have felt about it, she said he would have reveled in the "progress of America." She said that "even during Jackie's hardest moments," she never tried to protect him or "felt sorry" for him. Her ultimate compliment to the new president of the United States was the way she came to realize that Obama "didn't need her to feel sorry for him, either." She believes in him and his message of inclusiveness.

Jackie Robinson was neither a Democrat nor a Republican, but rather a highly visable citizen who was influenced by a politician's beliefs on issues and his or her willingness to fight for them. He especially respected Nelson A. Rockefeller, the four-term governor of New York, who braved public opinion by advocating and delivering large-scale human resources and drug rehabilitation programs. The Robinsons applauded his unprecedented support for public elementary, secondary, and higher education and his personal record of philanthropy.

Some newspaper columnists early on referred to Rachel as "the little lady behind the great man." She retorted, more than once, that she was "neither little nor behind him." She felt "powerful by his side as his partner, essential, challenged, and greatly loved."

Rachel has many memories of going to games at Ebbets Field and coming home after the games with Jackie, talking about "the game and the events of the day." She felt she "couldn't afford" to miss a home game and not share in "what was happening to Jack." She is forceful in reminding people that Jackie "was never a victim, and neither was she." She thought they were fortunate in having the opportunity to "make a difference." Rachel has never sought the spotlight, but she never shied away from it when the common good was at stake.

There are numerous quotes from the Robinsons, but one that especially resonates with me is when Jackie said, "life is not a spectator sport ... if you're going to spend your whole life in the grandstand just watching what goes on, in my opinion, you're wasting your life." Rachel reminds young people that baseball was "just a part" of Jackie's life. Len Coleman likes to quote his boyhood hero when saying, "A life is not important except in the impact it has on other lives." Coleman saw Robinson play and met him on several occasions in later life.

"He had intimidating skills, and he burned with a dark fire," famed author Roger Kahn once wrote. Dr. Bobby Brown, a third baseman for the archrival New York Yankees, played against Robinson in the World Series four times and marveled at his abilities to play the game. "He was quick and strong, and he never seemed to give up," Bobby, my predecessor in the presidency of the American League, has told me and others. He found Robinson to be "an engaging person" off the field.

One of my favorite quotes on Jackie Robinson came from Branch Rickey, his general manager of the Brooklyn Dodgers, who said there was "never a man in the game who could put mind and muscle together quicker than Jackie Robinson." Rachel quotes it from time to time.

Rachel Robinson takes enormous pride in Jackie's imposing feats as an athlete, many of which she witnessed, though she infrequently cites them in public. She recalls that he was the youngest of five children from Georgia and went on to be UCLA's first athlete to win varsity letters in four sports: baseball, basketball, football, and track. His athletic skills were legendary on the campus.

He was drafted into the United States Army in 1941 and assigned to Fort Riley, Kansas, where he learned that blacks with the same level of education as whites were not allowed to go to Officer Candidate School. He met heavyweight boxing champion Joe Louis during basic training and Robinson asked him for help. Louis contacted a friend in Washington, and Robinson and several other black men were then granted permission to train to become officers.

Robinson was commissioned as a second lieutenant and reassigned to Fort Hood, Texas, where he joined the 761st "Black Panthers" Tank Battalion. Upon leaving a hospital with an injured ankle, he boarded a bus with the wife of a fellow officer. The bus driver of the supposedly unsegregated bus line ordered Robinson to move to the back of the bus. Jackie refused, and the bus driver backed down. He was court-martialed and later acquitted by an all-white panel of nine officers. Injustice, wherever found, was something to be challenged, the young officer thought. He later remembered feeling angered and appalled.

In 1947, Jackie Robinson broke 60 years of segregation, often referred to as the "baseball color line." His extraordinary career began at a later age, so he had but a decade of play with the Dodgers. His career started with a bang, stirring long-held emotions on many sides of the racial issue.

During his electric tour with the Bums, as some reporters liked to call the Dodgers, he played in six World Series and six All-Star games. "He was in a class of his own," teammate and friend Pee Wee Reese once said, while another fellow Dodger and admirer Duke Snider thought Jackie was "the greatest competitor" he had ever seen. Even the Yankees were uneasy playing against Robinson because of his wide-open style of play, according to New York catcher Yogi Berra, who saw him as a constant threat to disrupt the defense.

Most baseball fans think of Jackie as a world-class second baseman, and yet he played his first season in 1947 at first base, earning the National League Rookie of the Year Award. He often said that he did not worry whether people liked or disliked him and that all he sought was "respect as a fellow human being."

Jewish baseball standout Hank Greenberg, who was no stranger to racial epithets in Detroit and Pittsburgh, and young Robinson once collided at first base, and he whispered something into Jackie's ear. Reporters were curious about what the legendary hitter had to say. "He offered me encouragement," Robinson said. Greenberg later said he told the Dodger rookie that the best way to combat slurs from the opposing team was to beat them on the field.

Two years later, Robinson was selected as the Most Valuable Player in the National League, the first black player so honored. During his breathtaking career, he batted .311, had 1,518 hits, and 137 homeruns. He compiled 125 stolen bases and had a .479 on-base percentage.

Jackie Robinson is often selected as the greatest second baseman in the history of the game, chosen over the likes of Rogers Hornsby, Eddie Collins, and Joe Morgan. One of his most enduring honors came on April 15, 1997, the anniversary of his debut, when Major League Baseball retired his jersey number, 42, across all MLB teams in recognition of his enormous contributions.

The unique recognition was the idea of Len Coleman, then NL president, and was supported by me as his AL counterpart. Commissioner Selig was quick to embrace the idea and he polled the owners, resulting in a unanimous vote of approval. President Bill Clinton joined the commissioner and Rachel Robinson at Shea Stadium in New York for the ceremony.

Rachel remembers being moved by the action that night, recounting the seemingly endless challenges that she and Jackie had faced over the years. Nothing of real importance comes easy or quickly, she thought.

Like his friend Larry Doby, the first African American to shatter the color barrier in the American League, he encountered the taunts of racism from many fans and even from some of his own teammates. He thought that some pitchers would attempt to throw at him and other players would sometimes try to push him off the base paths. And he was right.

Some Dodger players even threatened to sit out rather than play beside Jackie Robinson. Then manager Leo Durocher told the team that "he plays," and what's more, he can "make us all rich." For those players who did not need the added money, Durocher said he would arrange for their trades. The games went on.

"Mr. Robinson was the key to the integration of Major League Baseball," Doby, one of my special assistants in the American League, often reminded me. "One should not be confused about that fact." Doby especially admired what Jackie and Rachel Robinson had contributed to social justice after their time in baseball. "They were highly principled people," he said.

Virtually all blacks and many whites praised the entry of Robinson as "long overdue," but significant numbers of whites disagreed, many of them stooping to the use of verbal abuse. Most of the leading newspapers in America stood up for Robinson and the Dodger management.

Historians have long concluded that Robinson's integration and superior level of play served as a major blow to segregation in the United States and was a watershed in the eventual crumbling of other racial barriers. It was not easy; great things never are. Robinson spoke out against hotels and restaurants that would not allow him to stay and eat with his fellow Dodgers.

Some opposing players and crowds called Robinson a "nigger," but that kind of verbal abuse only served to unify the Dodgers in their resolve. Most Brooklyn players quickly saw Robinson, the person, not the color of his skin. In 1947, at the height of the heated debate, Pee Wee Reese put his arm around Robinson in response to fans that were shouting racial slurs at Robinson before a game in Cincinnati. The captain and shortstop of the Dodgers later said you can "hate a man for many reasons, but color is not one of them." Those actions, seen as symbols of racial tolerance, have become popular pieces of baseball folklore.

According to various press reports, the pressure seemed to taper off in 1948 and 1949 with several other black players now in the majors, like Larry Doby and Satchel Paige with Cleveland and three other players with Brooklyn. Jackie was joined by Hall of Fame catcher Roy Campenella and pitcher Don Newcombe, a hard-throwing right-hander who would go on to win 149 games. Robinson moved to his natural position at second base and led the National League in fielding. Many have forgotten just how good he was with a glove.

He won his only World Series championship in 1955, when the Dodgers beat the New York Yankees, though it was his worst year as a player. He was 37 years old and had missed 49 games because of injury. During his decade as a player, Robinson played on six World Series teams and was named to six National League All-Star Game teams.

He was inducted into the Baseball Hall of Fame in 1962, displaying grace through the spoken word and resolve to do more for the game he loved and the country he believed in. He felt he had just begun.

Don Newcombe joined Jackie and Rachel in advancing the cause of African American players during the 1950s. Once Robinson and Newcombe were denied admission to a five-star hotel in St. Louis, and Newcombe asked why. The manager said it was "the swimming pool where everybody socializes." Don explained they were ballplayers, not swimmers; the perplexed manager stammered and registered them. He and Larry Doby chuckled when they told me the story in my American League office in New York.

Significantly, Rachel Robinson has been honored at the White House by seven presidents, each of whom has thanked her for her stoic commitment to the common good. She is frequently quoted by members of Congress on matters of fundamental fairness. I believe she is a national treasure, a person who gains in luster with the passing of each year.

Rachel has rarely said no to deserving causes, especially ones that will advance the futures of deserving young people of color. Len Coleman has told me that she "cares and shares" and has never wavered "in causes for national good."

"The right of every American to first-class citizenship is the most important issue of our times," Jackie Robinson often said as he traveled the country in pursuit of universal equity. Rachel made many of those trips, and stood at his side with people like Dr. Martin Luther King, Jr. She often experienced hostility and grew stronger because of it.

She is frequently accompanied by her daughter, Sharon, an accomplished educator and author, who has reminded thousands of young people, through speeches and the printed word, of the relevance of her father's values and battles as they apply to the turbulent world around us. An important voice for Major League Baseball, Sharon has carried the Robinson message to schools and baseball parks in major and minor league cities for years. Through her efforts, the core values of the Robinsons are now incorporated in a program in the elementary school curricula in urban America.

For the 35th anniversary of the Jackie Robinson Foundation, an overflow crowd of friends, supporters, and celebrities jammed the ballroom at the Waldorf-Astoria. Rachel looked radiant that evening as she shook every hand in sight and offered a genuine smile of pride, joy, and appreciation.

Many in attendance, including individuals such as film director Spike Lee and actor Jimmy Smits, said she represented the values that "we as a society should embrace today." She was called "a true pioneer, like her husband," and an historic figure for the ages by some of the students who are Robinson Foundation scholars. One retired teacher from New Jersey, who saw Jackie play as a rookie first baseman, said Rachel has "unlocked the doors of hope for many promising young minds."

Comedian Bill Cosby and basketball titan Bill Russell were at the celebration to support the work of the Robinson Foundation, and Baseball Commissioner Bud Selig called it "a bastion for good."

It was an evening of promise and hope, a time to honor the lasting legacy of Jackie and Rachel Robinson. It was an opportunity to recognize an extraordinary woman who has spent a lifetime reaching out to others—often to the most unfortunate among us—and to one who has reminded millions of men, women, and children about the need to grow the human spirit.

It was a time of renewal for people of goodwill.

Bill
Veeck

Showman Veeck . . .

He once sent Eddie Gaedel to bat for his Browns.
Fans loved the St. Louis owner; other owners bristled.

For the
love of the game,
Bill Veeck

Fortunately for Major League Baseball, legendary owner Bill Veeck never grew up. He often whimsically reminisced about the joy he experienced as a youngster at quaint Wrigley Field: selling peanuts, hot dogs, and soda; manning a ticket booth; and listening to the fans. He even had fun working as a junior groundskeeper.

His father, William Veeck, Sr., once a Chicago sportswriter and columnist, had often written pointed articles about how he would run the Cubs, one of the National League's eight charter franchises, to make the team more successful. Finally the owner, William Wrigley, Jr., made him the president.

During his long tenure, William Sr., always in a starched shirt and necktie, gained considerable fame as, among other things, the person who decided to grow ivy at Wrigley Field. His son, Bill, actually helped plant the ivy and tended to it. Bill Veeck often said the ballpark on the north side of Chicago was his "home of choice" and the richness of the green playing field was a "soothing friend and companion."

In 1933, when his father died, Bill dropped out of college and went back to the Cubs where he eventually became club treasurer. He was a serious, though somewhat bored, student of baseball economics, but he understood the necessity for prudent fiscal management of the game.

In fact, Bill felt a need to know and understand every facet of the game if he were to ever change it for the better. He always thought that America's pastime was without many good stewards.

Young Bill Veeck had an unassuming air that was disarming to many of his older colleagues and later competitors. He liked to have fun—to think as a kid. He knew entertainment and he understood what kids wanted to experience at the ballpark in addition to a seriously played baseball game. Clearly, he was years ahead of most baseball people, and he raised the bar for those who would follow in ownership.

Bill Veeck spread his wings in 1941 when he left Chicago to purchase the Milwaukee Brewers of the American Association with former Cubs player and manager Charlie Grimm.

The partnership proved to be a successful one, both on and off the field. The franchise won three championships in five years, raising attendance to the highest level then known in the minor leagues.

While co-owner of the Milwaukee Brewers, Veeck served for nearly three years in the Marines during World War II, suffering serious injury that required the amputation of a foot. He learned to live with constant pain, but he was an unabashed patriot who believed in his country and its fundamental values, and believed that no sacrifice was too great for freedom.

Over the course of his adult life, Bill Veeck underwent 36 operations on the foot and on his leg above the knee. As an amusing aside to many of his friends, he had a series of wooden legs and, as a four-pack-a-day smoker, he used holes in them for ashtrays. This practice drew inquiring stares. Interestingly, he spoke against the use of tobacco.

Before leaving for the war, Veeck said he had tried to purchase the cash poor Philadelphia Phillies, but was denied by Commissioner Kennesaw Mountain Landis. Veeck wanted to infuse the Philadelphia roster with stars from the Negro Leagues, a move that would have engendered considerable controversy at the time. In recent years, some researchers have questioned the accuracy of the alleged acquisition attempt, which has become a part of baseball lore.

In 1946, Bill Veeck became the owner of a Major League Baseball team, the Cleveland Indians. He had a number of partners, something that slowed the approval of other club owners. One of his first acts was to put the team's games on the radio, a strategy that heightened interest in the Indians and quickly helped sell many more tickets.

It did not take Veeck and the Indians long to win.

In an effort to gain firepower in 1947, he signed Larry Doby as the first African American to play in the American League. A year later Veeck signed skilled Satchel Page to a Cleveland contract, making the lanky black pitcher the oldest rookie in major league history, though no one really knew his exact age. The best guess was that he was 42 years old at the time.

Doby told me that some of his teammates in Cleveland shunned him and refused to even play catch when he came to the majors. Doby struggled during his rookie season, getting only five hits in 32 at-bats. He was determined to improve, and improve he did, leading the remarkable Indians to the American League pennant and the World Series championship in 1948.

Doby suffered the same indignities that Jackie Robinson did in the National League. Robinson, the second baseman for the old Brooklyn Dodgers, beat Doby to the big leagues by less than three months, receiving considerably more media attention and national support than the understated Doby. Veeck never waivered in his unquestioned support of Larry Doby, his eventual friend for life.

Doby was an on-field assistant during my tenure as American League president (1994–2000). He was calm, cool, and thoroughly professional; he was, like few others, battle tested. He said Veeck was "the most courageous man" he ever knew.

Not everybody in Cleveland loved Veeck all of the time, especially when he signed black players and attempted to trade

popular player-manager Lou Boudreau to the St. Louis Browns
in 1947. The latter event caused heretofore unseen hysteria in
Cleveland, resulting in mass protests and countless petitions sup-
porting Boudreau. The press hammered the owner and Veeck
quickly recanted. He visited "every bar in Cleveland" to apologize
for "the lapse in judgment" and he assured fans at every stop that
the proposed deal was dead. Veeck later joked that he "drank a
lot of beer" on those tavern stops.

In response, the handsome Boudreau, a talented player with a
bat and a glove, led the Indians a year later to their first pennant
and World Series since 1920. His batting average was .355 and he
helped Cleveland establish a new major league season attendance
record of 2.6 million fans.

In 1949, Veeck and his first wife divorced and he was saddled
with an expensive settlement, forcing him to sell his valued
shares in the Indians. He left Cleveland a popular man and a compelling figure in Major League Baseball.

After selling the Indians, Veeck assumed perhaps the greatest challenge of his career. In 1951 he took on ownership of
the lowly St. Louis Browns. Respected sports columnist Jerome
Holtzman of the *Chicago Tribune* once told me that Veeck in-
herited the "dregs, a collection of old rags and tags." Veeck and a
small band of investors naively thought they could force the St.
Louis Cardinals out of town.

Veeck tried to rile the Cardinal ownership by hiring Cardinal greats Rogers Hornsby and Marty Marion as managers, and
Dizzy Dean as a radio announcer. He even decorated their shared
home, Sportsman's Park, with only Browns signs and memora-
bilia. Surprisingly, the National League entry had been a tenant of
the Browns since the 1920s, even though the Cardinals were by
far the more popular team.

Cardinal ownership became more and more resolute in face
of the harassment. They resented Veeck and the Browns.

After the 1952 season in St. Louis, Veeck proposed that the American League clubs share radio and television revenue with visiting teams. The owners said no, and Veeck refused to allow the Browns' opponents to broadcast games.

The League responded by eliminating the lucrative Friday night games in St. Louis, a crushing financial blow to the Browns. The real end came, however, when the Cardinals were sold to Anheuser-Busch. Veeck and his investors realized that the Cardinals now had deep pockets and a huge competitive edge.

Veeck tried to move the Browns to Milwaukee where they had played their first season in 1901, but AL owners balked. He then tried to locate the team in the sprawling Los Angeles market. Once again, the answer from the league was no.

In the meantime, Sportsman's Park was in need of expensive renovation since it no longer met code. Veeck was forced to sell the aging facility to the Cardinals and he was left without options, necessitating his sale of the controlling interest in the Browns. The franchise was transferred to Baltimore where baseball would flourish.

The man who thought "anything is possible" resurfaced in 1959 with an investment group that purchased a controlling interest in the Chicago White Sox, who went on to win their first American League pennant in 40 years and establish a record attendance of 1.4 million fans for home games. Comiskey Park was alive and well again, with boisterous fans reveling in the team's success.

Poor health forced Veeck to sell his share of the team in 1961, but he returned 14 years later for another tour as owner of the White Sox. He quickly drew the ire of his fellow owners when he and general manager Roland Hemond set up shop in a hotel lobby and made four trades in public view. Owners regarded him as a pariah, as one who had soiled their collective image over the years.

Only two weeks later, an arbitrator ushered in the age of free agency and the wealthier owners were clearly advantaged. Long the only owner without personal wealth, Veeck hung on for another five seasons in Chicago, surviving largely on his promotional wit, but his power began to wane.

Veeck used to tell Hemond, who was twice the Sporting News Major League Baseball Executive of the Year, not to prepare an annual budget because "we have no money." Hemond loved working beside Veeck who he believed was a genius and always made life challenging and novel. "We never stopped having fun," Hemond said.

Finding it impossible to compete financially in the free agency era, Veeck sold the White Sox in January 1981. He left the game disillusioned, seeing an increased emphasis on baseball as a business, not as family entertainment. The game was not fun for him anymore; he felt "out of it."

Bill Veeck had become a nationally known Major League Baseball owner and a one of a kind celebrity. He often railed against authority, which he viewed as lacking sincerity and compassion, putting him frequently at odds with the establishment in baseball.

Veeck was from a time when decency, originality, and respect for others, especially kids, really mattered. It was not unusual to find Bill Veeck espousing liberal and sometimes unpopular causes, both in and out of baseball. Although he had a wooden leg, he once participated in a daylong civil rights march at Selma, Alabama, without the use of crutches.

He genuinely liked and respected baseball players; two of his all-time favorites were power-hitting Hank Greenberg of the Detroit Tigers and smooth-swinging Harold Baines of the Chicago White Sox. Veeck had discovered Baines when he was a sandlot player at St. Michaels, Maryland, the off-season home of the Veecks.

Greenberg, who hit 58 homeruns in 1938, two shy of the Babe Ruth record, joined Veeck as a partner in the Cleveland ownership group. He became the Indians general manager and assembled a promising array of African American prospects for the Tribe. Greenberg finished his career with the Pittsburgh Pirates in 1947 and was one of the few opposing players to publicly welcome Jackie Robinson to the majors.

Baines played for five American League teams from 1980 to 2001. Yet he is best known as an outfielder and designated hitter for the White Sox, where he was recognized as one of the game's most consistent hitters, batting over .300 eight times. He is now a coach for the White Sox.

Bill Veeck spent his final years sitting in the bleachers at Wrigley Field, where baseball remained a game played under the sunlight and he always paid his own way.

He died in 1986 of a pulmonary embolism at age 71 and he was elected to the Baseball Hall of Fame five years later, an honor rarely accorded to an owner. Bill Veeck had to be smiling at the clear irony of the vote.

When the White Sox won their first World Series crown since 1917, beating the Houston Astros in 2005, owner Jerry Reinsdorf decided to give a coveted championship ring to Mary Frances Veeck, Bill's wife. "The Veecks are an important part of baseball history in the city of Chicago," he asserted. "We are grateful to them."

It was in Milwaukee that Veeck began to establish himself as a showman, as one who was willing to cross traditional lines for the amusement of fans. He always thought baseball was a unique brand of entertainment.

In his autobiography, *Veeck as in Wreck* (1962), Bill claimed to have installed a screen to make the right field target a little more difficult for left-handed pull hitters from the opposing team. The screen was on wheels so it could easily be moved to advantage the Milwaukee Brewers, Veeck later admitted. He had broken no rule by the ruse, but when discovered, the American Association passed an immediate rule to end the practice.

As in Milwaukee, Veeck never tired of promotions in Cleveland, nor did his many fans, young and old. He had, for example, a ceremonial burial of the 1948 pennant flag when it became apparent that his team could not repeat as champion in 1949, and he held a well-publicized "Good Old Joe Earley Night," staged for a fan who complained that Veeck was honoring everyone but the average "Joe." Veeck introduced fireworks displays after games, an activity that remains popular today at most ballparks.

Always the entertainer, Veeck launched a series of fan-friendly initiatives in cavernous Cleveland Municipal Stadium, hiring Max Patkin, a rubber-faced baseball clown, as a coach. The front office of the American League and Veeck's fellow owners were appalled and Patkin's time as a coach came to an abrupt end, even though the fans were delighted with his antics on the field. Max Patkin went on to become the "Clown Prince of Baseball," and he entertained in numerous major and minor league baseball parks before hoardes of adoring fans.

It was in St. Louis that Bill Veeck orchestrated some of his most memorable and bizarre publicity stunts, including the famous batting appearance on August 19, 1951, by midget Eddie Gaedel, and Grandstand Manager's Day, involving Veeck and Connie Mack and thousands of regular fans directing the entirety of the game via placards: the Browns won, 5-3, snapping a four-game losing streak.

After reading about the Gaedel appearance, an eleven-year-old kid from southwest Nebraska wrote Veeck and asked for an immediate tryout. Known for his soft spot for children, the owner told the eager youngster in a letter that he was a little too young, but he promised a tryout after high school graduation. "That kid was me," I told Larry Doby, and he smiled knowingly and said Veeck had told him the story long ago. He wrote many letters to wide-eyed kids who were certain they could help his Brownies.

The genius of Bill Veeck was seen by all when he introduced the first "exploding scoreboard" in the major leagues. It was an imposing 130-feet high and produced electrical and sound effects and shot fireworks whenever the ChiSox, as many reporters liked to call them, hit a homerun. Most major league clubs today have variations of the Veeck scoreboard, a popular sight and sound for the fans. He also added the players' names on the back of their uniforms, now a common practice among teams.

During this period of ownership, one of his most creative gimmicks was a bicentennial-inspired Spirit of '76 parade on opening day, featuring Veeck as the peg-legged fifer.

His "rent-a-player" scheme for taking stars from other clubs in their option years helped the White Sox win 90 games and finish third in 1977 behind leased sluggers Richie Zisk and Oscar Gamble.

In 1976, Veeck reactivated 54-year-old Minnie Minoso for eight at-bats so Minoso could say he had played in four decades. Four years later, he again reactivated Minoso who could then say he had played in five decades.

Perhaps Veeck's longest surviving idea was having storied announcer Harry Caray sing "Take Me Out to the Ball Game" during the seventh-inning stretch. His most copied idea was having players take curtain calls after hitting homeruns.

The 1979 season was his most controversial. With an assist from his colorful son Mike and a Chicago radio host, the White Sox held one of the most infamous promotions, Disco Demolition Night, which resulted in a riot at Comiskey Park and a forfeit to the visiting Detroit Tigers.

According to the younger Veeck, Mike, the president of the successful Charleston RiverDogs of the South Atlantic League, his father would never turn his back on children. "Everything he did included consideration of what kids might enjoy at the ballpark," he recalled. Mike tries to do the same as an innovator in minor league baseball.

During my presidency at Illinois State University, Bill Veeck accepted an invitation to visit the Bloomington-Normal campus and throw out the first pitch for a much-anticipated baseball series with Notre Dame. He captivated the fans and reporters with his good-natured candor and amusing baseball stories, and he signed autographs for everyone who asked throughout the game and sought the views of youngsters on school and the sport of baseball. He never stopped learning from the younger generation; they were his friends and future customers.

In striking ways, Mike is a replica of his famous father, always surrounding himself with bright young men and women who love the game and want to make it more enjoyable through creativity.

He said his dad "never graduated from anything," but he read constantly and liked to challenge others to think. Mike worked with his father for nearly six years on the South Side of Chicago, amassing knowledge and insight about baseball. Mike remembers his dad "always sought out and favored the working man" and that he deeply believed in universal education and civil rights.

"Dad was never judgmental," Mike recalled. "He gave everyone a fair chance." Mike especially admired that trait in his father.

The Veecks always knew associates by their first names and knew the contributions they had made. Mike is credited for a lot of the success of minor league baseball, a fun-loving entity that draws more than 43 million fans per year. As a co-owner of the RiverDogs, I can attest to the fact that he remains regularly sought out by peers who want to run ideas by him.

The Costas legacy,
Bob Costas

Some may believe Bob Costas invented sports broadcasting as we know it today. Not so. What he really did was reinvent and raise the bar on ways the major sporting events should be seen, reported on, and interpreted.

There were to be no shortcuts under his demanding mode for preparation and presentation, as he made his national presence known in the early 1980s on NBC Sports. Some of his colleagues even thought he regarded his profession as a calling, one that deserved and demanded no less than the ultimate in respect and commitment.

There was no one in the media game quite like Bob Costas in the 1980s, the energetic anchor and play-by-play person who had developed his skills in communications at Syracuse University. This man with a slender build thrived among the playing giants of baseball, football, and basketball. Star athletes seemed to welcome his penetrating questions because of his reputation for objectivity and fairness. He rarely ran out of challenging questions for representatives of management, much to their dismay and occasional discomfort.

Costas never tried to berate the individuals he interviewed; he wanted to bring out timely information and responses that would enlighten the audience. Nor did he ever knowingly intimidate anyone by the use of his well-known intellect. He had a unique way of putting his subjects at ease.

Bob Costas is very bright, a man who reads constantly and seeks out people, in and out of sports, who challenge him as a

He Knows Sports . . .

Bob Costas is perhaps best known for his reporting
of the Olympics and baseball for NBC Sports.

person and a professional. New and different ideas energize him, and he often likes to debate popularly held views in sports.

His thoughtful expressiveness and respect for those he meets have produced compelling moments. Costas likes many players in professional sports, but one of his all-time favorites was superstar Mickey Mantle of the New York Yankees. He admired his skills as a switch hitter and outfielder and his fan-friendly appearance on the diamond. At Mantle's funeral in Dallas, he gave a heartfelt eulogy before a jammed church of sports notables and regular fans. He said, "I guess I'm here, not so much to speak for myself as to simply represent millions of baseball-loving kids who grew up in the '50s and '60s and for whom Mickey Mantle was baseball. And more than that he was a presence in our lives—a fragile hero to whom we had an emotional attachment so strong and lasting that it defied logic."

After lecturing to my class at Princeton University several years ago, Costas was welcomed by the students, who thought he could have been a superior professor of English or History. His depth of ideas and use of words captivated them. "Mr. Costas could have been anything he wanted," said Chris Young, the all–Ivy League basketball and baseball player and a member of the class. Young graduated with honors and went on to pitch in the major leagues with the Texas Rangers and the San Diego Padres.

In a short time, Costas was known throughout the profession as one who reflected well-directed intelligence, thorough preparation, unusual articulation skills, unique insight, professional polish, and a touch of irreverence and wit. He introduced a new dimension to sports broadcasting. He was the "total package," according to Ken Shanzer, president of NBC Sports and a long-time associate.

Some in the press said young Costas was the new Howard Cosell, who had retired from ABC Sports as Costas emerged in the 1980s. Some likened the imposing vocabulary and presence of the two as sports commentators, but that is where the similarity ended. Costas projected an on-camera image of genuine interest and unquestioned sensitivity, whereas Cosell had built a reputation for being brash and, at times, overbearing.

People at 30 Rock have marveled at how Costas can identify with the older and the younger generations. For nearly 30 years, he has been successful, as few others in broadcasting, in bridging the often-large age gap.

And how has he done it? There appears to be no simple, single answer. In truth, there are several explanations for his extraordinary longevity at the top of highly competitive sports broadcasting.

In addition to a keen and inquisitive intellect, Bob Costas is interested in popular culture and always in touch with the times. He refuses to grow stale, having interests that regularly take him far beyond the world of sports. He has continually kept himself current and relevant, perhaps like few others in sports broadcasting, and he refuses to be typecast as many others in the media have been.

He is always curious, seeking out and testing popularly held ideas. He entices the bright among us with his well-spoken words and depth of thought. He is studied, but never boring. Regardless of the subject, he can inject humor and knowledge that appeal to people of all ages.

While he takes his work seriously, he refuses to take himself too seriously, even though he has strongly held views on social and political issues, and he is always attentive to others and their ideas. Friends—and I have been one of them for more than 20 years—enjoy his self-deprecating manner.

There are those, few in number, who believe Costas does not like to be challenged on air; that is hardly the case. Some of his best moments have been seen in curt exchanges with combative guests, like homerun king Barry Bonds of the San Francisco

Giants. Costas does not seek controversy, but he refuses to back away from it.

A few critics from the New York area believe that he wants to be more and more in charge at work, which is hardly surprising for an artist of his achievements. He has won an unprecedented 19 Emmy Awards in four categories—15 for outstanding sports host or play-by-play, two for writing, one for his late-night interview show, *Later ... with Bob Costas,* and one for feature reporting. He has also been nominated for an Emmy in journalism. Perhaps even more impressive is that he has been named National Sportscaster of the Year an unprecedented eight times by his peers, several of whom refer to him as "a legitimate star" in the business. Costas never cites or discusses his professional honors.

A few critics have heard that he has become tough to direct, sometimes showing signs of insecurity. One likened him to another NBC star performer, Johnny Carson, who dazzled when the red light of the camera was on, but was, in truth, somewhat shy when it went off. Costas knew Carson and admired his long and highly successful

Photo Courtesy of HBO

tenure on the *Tonight Show* at NBC.

In summary, the great majority of newspaper critics see him as consistently atop his game, on the highest pinnacle as a sportscaster, while a few others admit to his exceptional skill but add that "no one is perfect, not even Bob Costas." The latter journalists have few specifics to offer. Views of Bob Costas, especially from his media brethren, vary, but ever so slightly.

Malcolm DeWitt, sports editor of the *Post and Courier* in Charleston, South Carolina, believes Costas has "done everything you can do in sports broadcasting. Without question he is the best, and he has the awards to prove it. He was never shy about sharing his opinions on anything, but he never seemed overbearing."

Chuck Wooding, long-time sports columnist of the *Journal World* in Lawrence, Kansas, said he saw on Wikipedia that Costas was born on March 22, 1952, in Queens, New York. "If true, he will be 57 years old. He could easily pass for 35, and the last television star that could do that was Dick Clark (in his pre-Botox days, of course). He is, and has been, the most persuasive on-air voice in sports."

Don Walton, veteran columnist of the *Journal and Star* in Lincoln, Nebraska, said Bob Costas was "the only recent-day baseball announcer within reach of Vin Scully, and I still miss his baseball broadcasts. He always displayed respect for the game, a quality that is missing in today's high-profile national cable broadcasts. When he is part of any broadcast, the bar is raised."

Jim Rossow, sports editor of *The News-Gazette* in Champaign, Illinois, remembers Costas from his time in St. Louis, where he displayed a "unique passion" for sports in the community. "It was clear that he was on the path to stardom. My four kids and I feel comfortable listening to him, regardless of the sport."

Ron Blum, prominent baseball writer for the Associated Press in New York, thought long and hard about his response, concluding, "Listening to tapes of old NBC broadcasts, it is remarkable how well-prepared Bob Costas was and how interesting he was to listen to. It is a shame NBC lost interest in baseball, and that he hasn't broadcast games much during the second half of his career. While he's been acclaimed for his Olympics work, he could have been one of the great baseball broadcasters, following the likes of Mel Allen, Red Barber, Russ Hodges, Curt Gowdy, Vin Scully, and Jack Buck. He has a great feel for the historical rhythm of the game—too often missing in other contemporary broadcasters."

Laughing, Paul Beeson, the former president of Major League Baseball and the World Series champion Toronto Blue Jays, remembers that Costas wrote a book, *Fair Ball,* in 2000 and that its bestselling contents riled the establishment within Major League Baseball.

Indeed, Costas has been a thoughtful commentator on the state of baseball. In my book *The Inside Pitch ... and More,* I endorsed most of Costas's controversial revenue-sharing ideas, but disagreed with him on a few format questions.

Costas criticized the "lords of the realm" for not confronting and addressing the inadequate system of revenuc sharing that limited the chances of small-market teams to win. He believed at the time that baseball needed forward-looking leadership—men and women who were willing to take chances in the best interests of the game. His criticisms brought positive movement within the group of owners.

The commissioner of baseball and the owners have addressed much of what Costas pointed out nearly a decade ago, in terms of a far more relevant system of revenue sharing. He was highly critical of management and labor in his time-tested book, believing that both sides were putting the future of the game at risk.

An author of significant standing, Bob Costas has long been concerned with inadequate writing skills in the United States.

Costas accepted my invitation to work with the College Board's National Commission on Writing in calling widespread attention to the plight of the written word. He did public service announcements aimed at the young that reached a massive audience on local and national network and cable television. His work has resulted in more than two million dollars of airtime, advancing the message on the need for improved writing.

Bob and I also created grants for teachers of writing, recognizing exceptional educators who use innovative methods to inspire students to write. Their prize-winning methods are shared across the country through the publications of the College Board in New York City.

To really understand the depth of the Costas experience, one needs to roll the clock back to 1979 when he joined NBC sports. He has covered every major sport, but is most identified with the Olympics and baseball.

He has anchored prime-time coverage of the last five summer Olympics for NBC—Barcelona 1992, Atlanta 1996, Sydney 2000, Athens 2004, and Beijing 2008. He also hosted the winter games in Salt Lake City in 2002 and Torino in 2006. Reviews of his work have remained sky high over the years.

It should be pointed out that the Olympics have become a popular show of international athletic talent and a ratings and financial bonanza for NBC, and that Bob Costas has become a popular face of the spectacular competition. NBC showed the Olympics on prime time and on their two cable networks, MSNBC and CNBC.

According to NBC, he is scheduled to host coverage of the 2010 Vancouver winter games and the 2012 London summer games. He acknowledges being excited about reporting on future Olympic competition.

From 1983 through 1989, Costas teamed with former Yankee shortstop Tony Kubek on NBC's *Game of the Week* telecasts, and it was during this period of time that I began to know, understand, and respect his work. No one knows the game better than Bob Costas, who is at ease talking about the pitching strengths of greats Bob Gibson and Sandy Koufax or his love affair with old ballparks. He sees America's pastime as something unique and deserving of lasting preservation.

He hosted the network's *NFL Live* pre-game show for nine years (1984–1992), stepping aside following Super Bowl XXVII. He has been involved in the coverage of ten baseball league championship series and six World Series for NBC, and he has hosted five Super Bowls. Bob became the most recognized sportscaster in America during this hectic and productive era.

He returned to Major League Baseball in the 1990s, skillfully handling play-by-play for NBC and its All Star, playoff, and World Series telecasts. He became a visible part of baseball history, teaming with Hall of Fame second baseman Joe Morgan and the always-humorous Bob Uecker, voice of the Milwaukee Brewers.

His position within the game was one of earned respect, especially when he offered passionate commentary about baseball's history, appeal, and ongoing problems. Millions of fans valued his words, and he clearly influenced the sport through his incisive comments and masterfully worded essays. Bowie Kuhn, a former commissioner of baseball, called him "a poet."

One of my most controversial moments as president of the American League came when Roberto Alomar spit in the face of an umpire. My suspension and $100,000 fine were thought by many to be totally inadequate, and some fans and politicians even said that the Baltimore second baseman should have been forever banned from baseball. Costas and Morgan defended me, pointing out that I was compelled to uphold the collective bargaining agreement between the players' union and management. There is no doubt that their lucid on-air commentary cooled temperatures.

Bob Costas especially enjoyed being the play-by-play voice

of the NBA on NBC from 1997 through the 1999–2000 season and for many years prior was the host of NBC's NBA coverage. "Coaches and players liked listening to Bob," said Larry Brown, the Hall of Fame professional basketball coach and my NCAA championship coach at the University of Kansas in 1988.

While remaining with NBC, Bob Costas branched out to HBO Sports and Entertainment in 2001 and launched the critically acclaimed and Emmy Award–winning show *On the Record with Bob Costas,* later renamed *Costas Now.*

Costas had begun to diversify beyond sports as far back as 1988, serving as a substitute host for Bryant Gumbel on the *Today Show,* and then moving on to host his own late-night program, *Later … with Bob Costas.* The show, another Emmy Award winner, featured in-depth interviews exploring the lives of newsmakers, entertainers, and personalities from varied backgrounds that only occasionally included sports. He left the show after a five-year run, feeling fulfilled and optimistic about the future. He still contributes to the *Today Show* and the *NBC Nightly News.*

With the advent of NBC's *Football Night in America,* Bob Costas added still another chapter to his storied career in sports television. He hosts the prime-time Sunday night broadcast of top NFL games, which has included playoff games each season and two Super Bowls over six years. NBC's reentry into professional football has attracted an enormous following from all age groups.

Costas enjoys talking about one of his first jobs, at KMOX in St. Louis. "It was one of America's finest radio stations at the time and was an ideal place to learn," he found. He announced basketball games for the old Spirit of St. Louis in the ABA and for the University of Missouri.

Costas developed a lasting attraction to radio, returning to the medium in 1986 and launching the popular syndicated program, *Costas Coast to Coast.* The weekly, two-hour program ran for ten years.

Now, more than a decade later, he has returned to national radio, bringing his widely hailed show back with a new title, *Costas on the Radio,* keeping the old format of mixing interviews and commentary.

Over his long and productive past, Costas has been able to sit down and talk with varied icons such as Wilt Chamberlain, Yogi Berra, David Letterman, and Bruce Springstein. He has found each to be uniquely different and interesting.

You might reasonably conclude that Bob Costas thrives on people—people from all walks of life, people who dare to think aloud and outside of the conventional box. His intellectual curiosity and his versatility have served him well in a long and wide-ranging career.

A Popular Pair . . .
Autry and his horse, Champion.

The ultimate star,
Gene Autry

Millions of Americans knew Gene Autry as The Singing Cowboy, as the revered champion of western values and justice. He was a hero to men, women, and children alike, and his popularity for much of the 20th century was unrivaled.

He influenced the world of entertainment as no one else of his era and he counted presidents of the United States among his personal friends. Franklin D. Roosevelt and Lyndon B. Johnson were two of his favorites; these presidents sought him out for advice on matters of national significance. He also counted among his friends Richard Nixon, Gerald Ford, and Ronald Reagan.

Gene Autry was a patriot, first and foremost, and he understood the American people and knew what set his country apart from the rest of the world. He spoke with clarity on values and issues that affected the nation, whether controversial or not.

I was one of his followers as a schoolboy from southwest Nebraska, vigorously campaigning for him when the old Fox Theatre in McCook would have popularity contests after showing double features of Autry and Roy Rogers movies. The noisy voters seemed to side with Autry more often than not.

My parents even named me after the bigger than life cowboy, believing it might bring me luck. Gene was a popular name in 1939.

Later in life, after serving as a college president and professor for 23 years at three large state universities, I knew Gene Autry of the California Angels as one of the two Major League Baseball owners who had nominated me for the presidency of the American League. Ewing Kauffman, owner of the Kansas City Royals, persuaded Autry to join him in actively encouraging my candidacy and eventual election. The two were among the senior and most respected owners of teams at the time, and as Jerry Reinsdorf, chair of the presidential search committee and owner of the Chicago White Sox once told me, "you had the right people on your side."

Both Kauffman and Autry were impressed that their National League peers had chosen a president from a prestigious private university as their president, Bart Giamatti of Yale. Owners were impressed with his intellect and skillful use of words.

"Ewing and I liked the idea of having a college person and it would show our respect for education," Autry told me. Kauffman further believed that it would be beneficial to have a president from a public institution of higher learning, since Giamatti came from a private college. He noted that many state universities were located near American League cities.

Kauffman, a self-made billionaire from the pharmaceutical world, and I became close friends when I served as chancellor of the University of Kansas from 1981 to 1994. He appointed me to the boards of the Kansas City Royals and the Kauffman Foundation. We frequently talked, and occasionally argued, about important and evolving trends in elementary, secondary, and higher education and the mounting economic problems of baseball, long my favorite sport.

Kauffman liked to challenge associates by thinking outside of the box and reminding them that he "did not have time to be bored." The same was true of Autry.

It was a dream come true to have Gene Autry as vice president of the American League during my six years as president. Largely ceremonial, the position gave me an opportunity to really know the man. He was wise and humble and always willing to talk about any subject, but his eyes especially sparkled when recalling "the good old days" at Republic Pictures. He liked to laugh and it was contagious for the people around him.

He was especially fond of actors Smiley Burnette and Pat Buttram, regular sidekicks on his radio shows and in his movies, television shows, and rodeo tours. They amused and enlightened him. Gene Autry "never lost a friend" or so the story goes; it was a trademark for him in Major League Baseball.

Autry knew baseball, once having an offer to play the game for money as a young man. He recalled how he could hit the ball "a country mile." His later knowledge of the inner workings of the game was well known and widely respected by his associates.

Courtesy of Mrs. Gene Autry; Autry Qualified Interest Trust and the Autry Foundation

Gene Autry enjoyed going
to bat as a young man.

Autry would occasionally sing a song or two for the owners after an evening meal at their meetings around the holidays. George Steinbrenner, the often-controversial owner of the New York Yankees, usually made the request of his friend from California, and he would lead the applause afterward. Autry had a calming influence on Steinbrenner as few others had at the time in the circle of owners. Steinbrenner looked up to the cowboy; it was that simple.

For more than a decade in his prime, Gene Autry was more popular with movie fans than his close friend, John Wayne, who also spent much of his storied career at Republic Pictures. They shared many of the same conservative values and more than a few drinks. They were famous, but like most of us, flawed.

Gene Autry is, amazingly, the only performer to earn five stars on the Hollywood Walk of Fame for radio, recording, motion pictures, television, and live performance. The grandson of a Baptist preacher, he was born near Tioga, Texas, and spent his childhood and youth in various small towns in Oklahoma and Texas. His father was a wanderer, while his mother was sturdy as a rock. While still in his teens, he supported both of them along with his three siblings.

Autry was poor and had to drop out of his final year of high school, something he later regretted. At the age of 17 he went to work as a relief telegrapher for the Frisco Railroad in Oklahoma. He performed for his fellow railroad workers, who encouraged him. Will Rogers, who was from a small town in Oklahoma, was a star in those days and his example also inspired Autry to attempt a career in show business.

He began performing in 1928 on radio station KVOO in Tulsa, billed as the Oklahoma Yodeling Cowboy. The following year he traveled to New York City and made his first recordings for a number of labels. He was, in his own words, on his way. Autry would eventually become one of Columbia Records' most successful and long-standing artists.

He became country music's first genuine star, writing and recording hundreds of songs, which included nine gold records and one platinum record. His biggest hit was probably "Rudolph the Red-Nosed Reindeer," a song that he did not especially like and one that was recorded in a single take. It remains one of the top 20 in record sales every Christmas.

He preferred songs like "South of the Border," "Tumbling Tumbleweeds," "Mexicali Rose," and "Back in the Saddle Again," all major hits of the day.

His many movies, all B westerns, were credited with helping save the film industry in the 1930s. He opened the doors for many other performers while delighting millions of people as he rode his horse, Champion, another popular icon from the mid-1930s into the late 1950s. His Gene Autry Flying "A" Ranch Rodeo started in 1940 and attracted sell-out crowds all across America. It seemed to many that anything he touched turned to gold.

With the advent of World War II, the singing cowboy felt an obligation to his country and to his many fans to enlist in the armed forces. America applauded his actions; the head of Republic Pictures, Herb Yates, was irate.

Yates knew well that Gene Autry's movies at Republic Pictures were cash cows. His nearly 50 movies at Republic were all moneymakers, and Yates regarded him as a valuable franchise.

According to Autry, the studio head said he could arrange a military deferment, but Autry nixed the idea. Yates then threatened him with the likelihood of his career being destroyed by being out of the public eye and pledged to throw all of Republic's promotional might behind Roy Rogers. While Autry was serving his country, Rogers emerged as the new king of the cowboys, as Yates had warned.

Autry served as a C-47 Skytrain pilot in the United States Army Air Corps, flying dangerous missions between Burma and China as a member of the Air Transport Command. He wanted to be a combat pilot like his friend Jimmy Stewart, and he once asked Congressman Lyndon B. Johnson of Texas to help him get in the line of action. Johnson did, and this resulted in a long friendship.

Autry took enormous pride in his military service and remained close to those individuals with whom he had served during the conflict. "I have no regrets, only a sense of satisfaction," Autry often said about his time in the military.

Numerous national publications and elected officials applauded the sacrifice that Autry made for his country. He remained a popular national figure, and FDR was among his biggest fans.

Republic Pictures tried to pit Autry against Rogers without success. The two cowboys liked each other and bonded as lifelong friends, much to the dismay of Yates and his subordinates. The two often challenged studio executives and their edicts.

Autry always favored radio, the outlet that gave him his start. His weekly radio show on CBS, *Gene Autry's Melody Ranch,* was a huge success from 1940 to 1956. He enjoyed a successful run on television, too, with a weekly program.

Autry briefly returned to Republic Pictures after the war to finish out his contract, but soon moved to form his own production company to make westerns, which would be released by Columbia Pictures, beginning in 1947. He said he found peace with the change.

He also starred in and produced his own television series on CBS beginning in 1950, becoming the first major western movie star to start his own television production company and star on TV. The series, like most of his other ventures, was an immediate success and a big-ticket item. His fans appreciated him on any size screen.

He hung up his spurs as a performer in 1964, having achieved top billing in nearly 100 films and on more than 600 records, an unprecedented feat.

At one time, his various companies employed thousands of people and he remained close to show business, buying a ranch near Newhall-Santa Clarita, California, that he named Melody Ranch. Many B westerns and television serials were filmed there, including the early years of *Gunsmoke* with James Arness.

He never forgot the Cowboy Code, which he developed after World War II for his young fans. In truth, he tried to live by these "commandments" and he often recited the ten rules to his radio and television audiences. They were:

The Cowboy must never shoot first, hit a smaller man, or take unfair advantage;

He must never go back on his word, or a trust confided in him;

He must always tell the truth;

He must be gentle with children, the elderly, and animals;

He must not advocate or possess racially or religiously intolerant ideas;

He must help people in distress;

He must be a good worker;

He must keep himself clean in thought, speech, action, and personal habits;

He must respect women, parents, and his nation's laws; and

The Cowboy is a patriot.

But Gene Autry was not perfect, sometimes failing to measure up to his oft quoted commandments. Certain of his closest friends feared that he was drinking too much near the end of his career as a performer and some worried about his "reputation as a ladies' man." The handsome Autry was a magnet for young and attractive women, especially when he toured with his rodeo. The same can be said for many of today's stars of movies and television.

Autry clearly battled his demons, but according to award-winning biographer Holly George-Warren, he emerged "in a positive light as one of America's most charitable benefactors, known for his boundless generosity, and as a patriot who enlisted in World War II." He was an immensely personable man with an army of friends who always remained loyal to him and were poised to defend his every action.

Stunningly, he gave deserving charities some $250 million, and his trust still provides more than $6 million a year for deserving causes. He was a man who knew how to reach out to the deserving, whether they were young or old. No one of his theatrical era rivaled or even came close to his generosity. Only actor Paul Newman played in his charitable league and that was many years later.

In 1932 he married Oklahoma native Ina Mae Spivey. She was an intelligent woman with a knack for business who served as her husband's behind-the-scenes advisor. She died in 1980.

Autry's second wife, Jacqueline Ellam, has played a major role in managing the Autry businesses including the California Angels. She is known for her financial acumen and willingness to make difficult decisions. Fittingly, Jackie Autry today serves as honorary president of Major League Baseball's American League.

Neither marriage resulted in children.

When Major League Baseball announced plans to add an expansion team in Los Angeles in the 1950s, Autry, a minority owner of the minor league Hollywood Stars, expressed an interest in acquiring the radio broadcast rights to the team's games.

According to legend, Autry's approach was so sincere, thoughtfully worded, and persuasive that he was talked into becoming the owner of the franchise rather than simply a broadcast partner. "That has only happened once in the history of MLB," Commissioner Bud Selig noted. "Gene was the right person at the right time. He was perfect."

The team was initially named the Los Angeles Angels in 1961. When the team moved to suburban Anaheim in 1966 it was called the California Angels. It was labeled the Anaheim Angels from 1997 until 2005 when it became the Los Angeles Angels of Anaheim.

Gene Autry thoroughly enjoyed owning the Angels and

knowing his players on a first name basis. He liked to visit with the manager and players in the dugout. Reggie Jackson, a member of the Baseball Hall of Fame and a former Angel, said Autry was a hero to him and his teammates.

Autry never missed a home game. His wife Jackie said he was a kid at the ballpark and he always kept a scorecard. He said little during a game because he was engrossed with the action on the field.

The Autrys made the painful decision to sell the Angels to the Walt Disney Company in 1995, believing the economics of the game gave teams like theirs little chance to win on a consistent basis. It was a unique opportunity for me as the American League president to observe Mrs. Autry and Michael Eisner firsthand during the sale process. She was resolute and organized; he was smooth and corporate in attitude and manner.

Included for many years on *Forbes* magazine's list of the 400 wealthiest Americans, Gene Autry amassed a fortune by acquiring valuable radio and television properties in Arizona, California, and other states. He also proved to be a shrewd real estate investor in the Los Angeles area.

The cowboy never understood why so many people made a fuss over him at the baseball games. He was not the star, the players were the stars. He remained humble and self-effacing until the day he died on October 2, 1998, at age 91. Gene Autry was the ultimate star and millions of fans knew it.

Bob Gibson . . .

His number 45 is retired in St. Louis.

"You want Gibby on
your side,"
Bob Gibson

Sometimes you learn what you need to know about an individual after an initial visit; other times it is not that simple.

I first met Bob Gibson at a University of Nebraska football game in the 1970s when I served as chief of staff to the Chancellor, who knew of my affection for baseball and my admiration for the St. Louis Cardinals pitching ace. It was a choice assignment for me and many of the university staff in Lincoln were envious.

Gibson arrived several minutes after the Huskers had scored the first touchdown. Nebraska was a national force in college football at the time, and the Bob Devaney–coached team scored many touchdowns during his colorful era.

I can still picture Gibson stepping off the elevator to the press box, dressed in black slacks, a gray turtleneck sweater, and a leather jacket. Heads turned. The center of attention had arrived.

Accompanied by Charles Washington, an African American journalist from the Near North Side of Omaha, Gibson said little at the outset, as many in the press box walked by him to see up close the most famous professional athlete in Nebraska history. Gibson politely refused to take an assigned seat as he fixated on the field of play.

He seldom smiled, looking as advertised—somewhat menacing, and he showed little interest in small talk. He resembled a well-coifed lion. A reporter from the *Omaha World-Herald* came by with a question, which Gibson answered in a matter of seconds before turning his attention back to the game. He might as well have been wearing a "do not disturb" sign.

Only the governor of Nebraska, Norbert T. Tiemann, received a firm handshake and that was because Washington insisted, emphasizing that the governor was sensitive to the concerns of the black community. Gibson admired Charles Washington and what he was trying to accomplish for minorities in Omaha.

With the start of the second half, Gibson began to ask me a few questions. It was readily apparent that he admired Coach Devaney and his compulsion to win. He especially respected the players on the defensive side of the line, then known as the Black Shirts, who were among college football's most tenacious athletes.

He mentioned Tom Osborne. He liked the way the Nebraska coaches were now recruiting from the Omaha area, losing few of the city's best prospects at the time. Gibson did not understand how the Huskers had let Gale Sayers, the consensus All-American from Omaha, get away to neighborning Kansas.

Early in the fourth quarter, I offered to take Gibson and his companion to the Nebraska dressing room to talk with Coach Devaney, then thought to be the ultimate invitation in the state of Nebraska. He politely declined, making his way out of the press box. Two insistent fans stood in front of the elevator, holding National League baseballs and asking for autographs. He signed them on the way down.

As he departed, he paused long enough to offer a sincere handshake, express his gratitude, and say that he would welcome an opportunity to talk baseball again in the future. I had posed several questions he found insightful. My memory of that experience still burns bright, as it would for any true baseball fan.

Years later in 1995, as president of the American League, I named Hall of Famers Larry Doby of the Cleveland Indians and Bob Gibson of the Cardinals as two of my on-field assistants. As such they had considerable influence on decisions about how the game should be played. They were especially effective in advising me on matters of player discipline and acceptable standards.

Ron Blum, the long-time baseball writer for the Associated Press in New York, questioned my naming a National League legend as an AL advisor. "He's from Nebraska," I answered. The question was never raised again.

Gibson was a sensational hire for Major League Baseball, a real asset to the game. He was a teacher and interpreter of the game and his insights were unique and hard-hitting. Bob never learned how to pull a punch, much to the amusement of our staff.

In disciplinary meetings with players and managers, Gibson was both articulate and stern. He never minced words, often to the surprise of the principals in the room. After all, he was Bob Gibson, one of the most celebrated pitchers in the history of the game. No one misinterpreted him or where he was coming from. He was open and fair.

Managers in the American League were especially pleased when he went on the field before games and conversed with them. Both they and the players accorded him with genuine respect. A couple of them even wanted his autograph.

Joe Torre, former manager of the New York Yankees, always reminded me of my good fortune to have Gibson at my side. "Gibby was the best there was," Torre often said, reminding me that he played with him in St. Louis.

Remembering the first time he saw Bob Gibson pitch, Torre, now manager of the Los Angeles Dodgers, told me that "when necessary, he had three pitches …fast, faster, and fastest."

He also said, "I never met a hitter who looked forward to facing Gibby … never."

Gibson was "hungry" and "lived for success on the field," Torre added. "He is a close and lasting friend who is totally honest."

It is highly unfortunate, I believe, that Bob Gibson was never given a major league position in a front office or somewhere at the administrative level. Perhaps he was too blunt for many in the sport and perhaps the color of his skin was an unspoken factor, especially in the early days after his playing career ended.

Many of us still remember Gibson as he was in his prime as a methodical marvel for St. Louis. He was a money player, seeming to reach untested heights during the World Series. He sometimes defied description as a world-class athlete.

In 1968, Bob dominated the National League hitters—sluggers like Willie Mays, Hank Aaron, Roberto Clemente, and Ernie Banks. His earned run average was a stunning 1.12, unmatched in modern baseball history. "Gibby threw smoke in those days," Bob Broeg, veteran sports editor of the *St. Louis Post-Dispatch,* once told me. "His fast balls and sliders defied description and left many a hitter in denial. Bob Gibson was the greatest competitor to ever pitch."

Gibson thought Hank Aaron despised pitchers "nearly as much as I despised hitters." Gibson went up against some of the game's marquee pitchers, artists like Juan Marichal of the San Francisco Giants, Tom Seaver of the New York Mets, Denny McLain of the Detroit Tigers, and Sandy Koufax and Don Drysdale of the Los Angeles Dodgers.

"We all threw hard and threw sliders and hit the corners and moved the batters off the plate to make certain they understood who was setting the agenda," Gibson explained in his autobiography, *Stranger to the Game.*

Gibson especially enjoyed competing against Drysdale and Koufax of the Dodgers, believing that Drysdale was somewhat like him in attitude and talent, but meaner, and that Koufax was the "nicest of the bunch," but could be tough as nails when the outcome of a game was in doubt.

During the Gibson era and before, owners discouraged their players from becoming too friendly with the opposition. Even Joe DiMaggio of the Yankees kept distance from his kid brother, Dominic, when he played outfield for the rival Boston Red Sox. Now many of today's players are friends with those wearing different jerseys.

Torre, a managerial legend, once said he would not describe Gibson as unfriendly when he pitched. "Hateful was more like it," he asserted. His former Cardinal teammate, Curt Flood, said Gibson pitched "with a chip on his shoulder."

Among his best friends were teammates from the championship 1964 Cardinals—Tim McCarver, Lou Brock, Ken Boyer, Mike Shannon, Bob Uecker, Curt Flood, and Bill White, who became the first African American president of the National League. It was the Redbirds first World Series in 18 years.

In that Series, Gibson and his brash teammates especially enjoyed topping the Yankees, and playing in historic Yankee Stadium, "the kind of place that brings out a player's best." The native Nebraskan liked pitching to Mickey Mantle, Roger Maris, and Yogi Berra, and his 31 strikeouts set a World Series record.

Manager Johnny Keane knew how to motivate Bob Gibson, almost as well as Gibson's oldest brother, Josh, when they were growing up. After the

Hall of Fame Photo

Many never caught up with his fastball.

memorable World Series victory, Keane said his pitching star "didn't pitch only with his arm; he pitched with his heart." After the historic World Series victory, Gibson was flown to Omaha on a chartered plane and honored with a motorcade and parade, the first such tribute in his hometown for a man of color.

When Bob was born in 1935, he was the youngest of seven children. His father, a cabinetmaker, died of tuberculosis several months before his birth and his mother worked at a laundry and also cleaned at houses and hospitals to make ends meet. The family was poor, so poor that they did not own a camera, and thus there is no picture of his father.

Josh assumed many of the adult responsibilities at home, and he became a model for his youngest brother and other youngsters in the ghetto of Omaha. Josh earned a degree from Creighton University in Omaha and wanted to be a teacher and coach, but at the time there was no suitable job for a young college graduate who was black. Disillusioned, he organized neighborhood kids into athletic teams at a local recreation center.

Early on, basketball was young Bob Gibson's best sport. He was good, good enough that his five brothers permitted him to play with them. The Gibson boys challenged all comers.

Much of Bob's interest in sports was the result of Josh's excellent coaching. He actually feared failure because of Josh and his commitment to excellence. Josh was always watching, or so Bob thought.

In 1947, Jackie Robinson broke the color barrier and joined the Brooklyn Dodgers. That development inspired young Gibson to believe he could become a professional athlete. He did not know at the time which sport best suited him, basketball or baseball.

In the meantime, Josh's teams kept on winning, and Bob was a significant ingredient in those victories. The older Gibson had no time for losing. In 1951, when Bob was 15 years old, his

American Legion baseball team became a Nebraska state champion. Still, basketball remained his best sport.

A few weeks before college was to start, the athletic director at Creighton University, a stone's throw away from the projects, recruited Bob Gibson to play basketball with the Blue Jays. Bob knew little about Creighton basketball, other than that its ranks were filled with white players. What mattered was the offer of a full athletic scholarship and a chance to get an education and play basketball.

Bob's enthusiasm for his classes fell far short of the enthusiasm he showed on the basketball court. He was the first black to attend the Jesuit school in Omaha on a basketball scholarship, and he would be a starting guard as a sophomore. He was compared to the great Elgin Baylor. Despite making honorable mention All-American and establishing a new school scoring record, he failed to establish himself as a professional prospect.

He later became the first member of the Creighton Sports Hall of Fame, largely for his basketball feats. Prize-winning columnist of the *Omaha World-Herald,* Wally Provost, called Gibson "the fiercest competitor" ever seen on the Omaha sports scene.

Bob Gibson then set his sights on professional baseball, even though he had no special niche. He played both the infield and the outfield in college, and occasionally he pitched. He led the Nebraska College Conference with a .333 average as a switch hitter.

His pitching was somewhat erratic, though he had a 6-2 record his senior year. He had the raw skills and decided during his last year at Creighton to concentrate on baseball. And since MLB seemed stocked with black outfielders, he decided to pursue pitching.

Since the Cardinals showed a continuing interest in him, he signed a contract with St. Louis for a thousand dollars, played out the season for three thousand, and then joined the Harlem

Globetrotters for four months at a salary of a thousand a month. He roomed with Meadowlark Lemon, who found Gibson to be talented, thoughtful, and serious.

During his time with the Cardinals from 1959 to 1975, he registered extraordinary achievements, many never seen before or since. Considered the best pitcher in St. Louis history, he dominated with a blazing fastball, a razor-sharp slider, and a deceiving looping curveball. He was known to throw close, fast inside pitches, but he had excellent control and hit only 102 batters in his 16-year career, far fewer than Don Drysdale of the Dodgers.

The right-hander won 251 games and lost 174, posted an eye-popping 2.91 earned run average, and struck out 3,117 batters. He made eight National League All-Star teams, won two World Series, and earned an amazing nine Golden Gloves for his defense.

He was awarded the World Series Most Valuable Player Award in 1964 and 1967, and won Cy Young Awards in 1968 and 1970. In 1968, he registered the lowest earned run average in 54 years.

Many forget that Gibson was also a good hitter who was sometimes used by the Cardinals as a pinch hitter. In the 1970 season, he hit .303, which was 100 points higher than the team's regular shortstop. He hit 24 career homeruns and two more in the World Series, and he batted in 144 runs. He was even used as an occasional pinch runner.

Admittedly, Gibson could be brusque and surly even with his own teammates. Catcher Tim McCarver laughs when telling about Gibson brushing off a sign, saying, "The only thing you know about pitching is you can't hit it." Gibson and McCarver have remained best friends over the years.

Another close friend, first baseman Bill White, told me "you want Gibby on your side in case of trouble." White was especially pleased when I appointed Gibson to the American

League position.

Never known for a smile or excessive laughter, I found Bob Gibson to be a man of enormous humility and great loyalty. He was one to side with on matters of principle. It is only right that his number 45 will never be worn again by a member of the St. Louis Cardinals and that he was voted to the Major League Baseball All-Century Team. He will be remembered as one of the most intimidating pitchers of all time.

What I value most about my time with Bob was learning, firsthand, the importance of perfection as a professional, the often forgotten role of leading by example, and the lessons of what must be learned from the ghetto of Omaha. Bob Gibson is my friend and, in some ways, a mentor.

Oakland A's Photo by Michael Zagaris

Billy Beane . . .

He always had time for a player.

The magic of
Moneyball,
Billy Beane

Many in the Bay Area regard Billy Beane as a rock star, as one whose magical skill gives them something to believe in, something to cheer about during the summer months.

In an area rich in sports lore, the vice president and general manager of the Athletics is today, arguably, the most prominent sports figure in the Oakland and San Francisco expanse. The cities by the bay have produced stars such as Willie Mays and Barry Bonds, Rickey Henderson and Dave Stewart, Joe Montana and Jerry Rice, Bill Walsh and Tony LaRussa.

Over the past decade, Beane has fielded consistent winners with low payrolls. He has long intrigued other general managers and owners, but it was not until 2003, when Beane was featured in Michael Lewis's best selling book *Moneyball,* that he burst onto the national stage.

The much-quoted book laid out his methods and how he used sabermetric principles to run his team in a cost-efficient way. Lewis Wolff, a Los Angeles real estate developer who bought the A's in 2005, explains that Beane can quantify and analyze data to help him make informed decisions that traditionally have been made subjectively. "He identifies the objective variables more than most people in baseball do," Wolff says.

That was the essence of *Moneyball.* According to Wally Haas, a former owner and chairman of the Oakland A's, Beane changed Major League Baseball forever with his somewhat unorthodox and analytical practices.

Other owners demanded that their general managers move

with dispatch to understand and consider employing Beane's techniques, believing some modification of them could enhance their own chances of winning at a lower cost. Other GMs were irritated and perplexed; unsurprisingly, Beane caused uneasiness and anxiety among his peers. Even Commissioner Bud Selig studied the Oakland approach for success. "Billy Beane can be very persuasive," Selig told me.

According to the book, which will be made into a motion picture, Beane's methods have influenced the way clubs, players, and owners in the national pastime think about the game. Even

with his deep pockets, Yankee owner George Steinbrenner had his subordinates learn what they could from the book to strengthen their operations in New York. Steinbrenner was impressed when billionaire Warren Buffet scanned the book and found it an instructive read, and the Omaha investor does know baseball.

The old-school baseball establishment felt under siege because they tended to side with traditional approaches to the game—the

Oakland A's Photo by Michael Zagaris

ones they knew, understood, and

Billy Beane proved you can win on a limited budget.

practiced. In the past, they argued, these methods had worked for the betterment of baseball and massive changes were not needed; perhaps they were even dangerous, the skeptics said.

Quite candidly, the bestseller had become a sore point with a growing number of both general managers and their scouts, who felt increased pressure from ownership to produce fast and more measurable results. Beane's stock continued to soar nationally with huge sales of the book. It was a smash hit with national talk shows.

Even those in business and industry wanted to hear more about the successful approach in Oakland, and they paid a lot of money for presentations by Billy Beane. He was in demand everywhere, and five years after the book's release, Beane still makes some 30 appearances a year, speaking about his use of undervalued assets to gain a competitive edge.

The lanky A's official even made a presentation to the Deutsche Bank in Paris last April. Wally Haas points out that Beane is a popular candidate for corporate boards, as business is ever seeking new and better strategies to increase profits.

Beane says he enjoys the speaking circuit, saying that he finds it exhilarating and that it allows him to branch out beyond the realm of baseball. "It forces me to think in new and different ways," he has explained. He especially enjoyed having Warren Buffet ask him a few challenging questions.

He now works directly with Oakland owner Lewis Wolff in another venture outside of baseball. Wolff purchased an expansion Major League Soccer team in 2006, the San Jose Earthquakes, and Beane is assisting him in the use of some of the same strategies he employs with the Athletics. Beane is a fan of the sport of soccer and clearly believes in its long-term possibilities.

One project that is central to the future of the Athletics is the realization of a new ballpark. Cost-conscious public officials have been reticent. Beane, always appearing cool and collected, is the one who makes the public case for the baseball-only facility. The old Coliseum, which is cavernous and also home for the Oakland Raiders, is far from ideal for baseball, with so many of the seats far away from the playing field.

"One cannot expect the A's to compete indefinitely without a new facility like the ones other MLB teams enjoy," Commissioner

Bud Selig told me. A new ballpark in the next three to five years would mean an instant jump in interest, attendance, and revenue, Beane contends.

Not surprisingly, Wolff is threatening to leave the Oakland area, quoting an array of persuasive facts and figures. Other owners who have been successful in getting new ballparks, have employed the same hardball strategy. The San Francisco Giants, archrival of the A's, have a new state-of-the-art ballpark, one that has become a favorite with fans in the Bay Area.

A lifetime resident of the Bay Area and a member of the prominent family that owns Levi Strauss, Wally Haas believes it is naïve to think the Athletics can survive indefinitely in the Coliseum. He has long favored a new venue, one that will give the franchise adequate revenue to compete and keep some of its emerging standouts. The Haas family owned the Oakland club for 15 years, and they were especially popular with the baseball community.

Many have wondered why Beane, with all his acclaim, has stayed in the East Bay as general manager of the A's, a small market team. That is surprising to many in the media because managing a small market team is a continual struggle, and he has been offered millions of dollars to do his thing elsewhere.

The Boston Red Sox contacted Beane in November of 2002 and offered him a five-year, $12.8 million contract and a house in southern California to become their general manager. He would have had one of the game's largest budgets to compete in the always-tough Eastern Division of the American League. Even television anchor Katie Couric, then a companion of owner Tom Werner, called to encourage Beane to consider the job.

The opportunity to work for one of MLB's most historic franchises and have financial security was too good to pass up, so Beane signed on—for a day.

He changed his mind the next morning, and has not regretted it since. "Not for a moment," he told me. Other clubs have tried to hire him too, but the answer has always been the same.

Soon after Wolff bought the A's in 2005, Billy was given equity in the franchise (reportedly four to five percent) and a lengthy contract extension. He always wanted to be a part owner—someone with an economic stake in the performance of the team.

For now, the A's need not worry about losing Beane. He is in his comfort zone, Wally Haas has assured me, and Beane and Haas have remained close friends over the years.

A native of California, Beane especially likes the pace of life in the northern part of the state. The general manager of the A's, with Hollywood good looks, has been known to go to work in shorts and sandals and be accompanied by his border collie. Though he is widely recognized, the people of Oakland and San Francisco give him his space, approaching him from time to time, but always in a friendly and supportive way.

His signature mode of operation with the A's—making bold trades and realizing exceptional results out of a meager budget— has caught many an eye during his 10 years as GM. He has been with the American League entry for two decades, having learned the business from one of the best, Sandy Alderson, who went on to a key management position in Major League Baseball.

Beane and Alderson are both sons of career military officers, but that is where the similarity appears to end. Alderson is a former Marine officer, a graduate of the Harvard Law School and a button-down shirt kind of person. Sandy laughs, but not a lot. Alderson and Beane have always liked each other; they both respect the other's views, insight, and values on baseball matters. "I learned a lot from Sandy," Billy often says. "He was a skilled mentor."

No one today believes more in the value of a college educa- tion than Billy Beane, who frequently takes time to encourage youngsters in that direction.

In high school, Beane was an exceptional athlete at
Mt. Carmel High School in San Diego, and he had a lot going for
him. Stanford University saw him, for example, as its quarterback, but the New York Mets selected him in the first round of
the 1980 amateur baseball draft. He signed with the Mets, but it
was the start of a lackluster playing career.

Beane played parts of six seasons in the major leagues as
a reserve outfielder, with the Mets, the Minnesota Twins, the
Detroit Tigers, and finally the Athletics. He was on the bench for
two wins in the World Series—with the Twins in 1987 and with
the A's in 1989. But Beane went to school during those years in
professional baseball, learning lessons that would serve him well
as an administrator. Nothing of importance escaped his eye, and
some in the game would award him an honorary doctorate for
his achievements as a general manager.

For example, Beane told me that he immediately saw firsthand the value of second-tier ballplayers who outhustled others
who were thought to be potential big league stars. As a scout
for the A's, he was given the chance to "build more than merely
maintain." He learned the importance of using objective data in
player development and he soon found that administrative survivors rely on data, not on the gut impressions of scouts.

"We have the ultimate challenge in Oakland," Beane admits.
"We are required to reshape our team every year because of financial restraints." Billy Beane is expected to compete with other
teams that spend two to three times more than his A's.

Beane and his young associates thrive on daring trades, often
involving players on the verge of free agency. "They are about to
become too expensive for us to keep because of our budget limi-
tations," Beane explains, without emotion. It is what it is.

He takes pride in his aggressive associates who he includes in
any serious discussion about player personnel. He believes they

are fast and creative learners who are likely to climb the steep ladder to baseball success. Beane especially enjoys the midseason trading deadline which can make or break a team like Oakland. Pizza is the only menu option for days at a time for Beane and his noisy late-night crowd.

"The challenge for the Oakland A's never ends," Beane has told me. Though known for his blockbuster trades, Beane is quick to point out that the clear objective is to multiply the number of outstanding prospects, young players who have a good chance to make it to and in the big leagues. He has brought in established players like Johnny Damon, Cory Little, Jermaine Dye, and Billy Koch for short periods of time.

Oakland players believe in their general manager and his unique way of doing things.

Not all of Beane's trades have worked out, to be sure. The much-publicized deal that sent ace pitcher Tim Hudson to Atlanta netted three players for Oakland who have contributed nothing to the Athletics. Many Oakland fans were annoyed with the trade and were openly critical, but they never lost confidence in their general manager. "Fans trust Billy Beane to be right most of the time," Haas told me. The A's have weathered the loss of some of the game's greatest talent.

Sports are important to the people in the Bay Area, Beane explains. "But sports represent only a part of life. The fans have unusual perspective out here." He said that he is anything but envious of his colleagues in major cities like Boston and New York, adding, "Their lives are miserable much of the time with a never relenting media."

Regrets are few for Billy Beane, but he does wish that he could have taken Stanford to the Rose Bowl as its quarterback, and he wishes that he had a framed college diploma hanging on his office wall at the Coliseum.

What the broad-shouldered, six-foot-four executive wants

now is a World Series championship for the A's, a nucleus of young standouts at each position, a new first-class ballpark, and a full life in an open-minded community rich in sports, literature, and the arts. Beane sees the Bay Area as the ideal place for dreaming and realizing those dreams, however ambitious.

Always a
Mountaineer,
Jerry West

Jerry West remembers playing basketball as a kid in the hills of West Virginia. Nothing stopped him. He braved wind, rain, and even snow. Often he played until his hands were bleeding.

His basketball court in those days could be found at a neighbor's house in Cheylan, West Virginia, where a partially bent hoop had been nailed to a storage shack. He came from humble beginnings, the son of a coal mine electrician who made just enough to support six children, and who had little time or energy to engage his son in sports.

Jerry remembers being a shy youngster who was small and frail and needed vitamin injections. His parents kept him away from sports, fearing a possible injury. When Jerry was 12, he lost his closest brother in the Korean War, and he never totally recovered. He became more and more of a loner... devoting much of his time to fishing, hunting, and basketball. Jerry later admitted that he had become "obsessive."

West attended East Bank High School from 1952 to 1956. He became the basketball team's starting forward and developed into one of West Virginia's finest prep basketball players. West was named All-State from 1953 to 1956, and then All-American in 1956 when he was selected the state's Player of the Year. He was known for his jump shot, hustle, and focus. He often skipped meals to practice.

West remembers that more than 60 universities expressed an interest in him, but he knew where he wanted to go, where he would feel at home—West Virginia University. The citizens were

Courtesy of West Virginia University Department of Athletics

As a Los Angeles Laker . . .

Jerry West scores two of his more than 25,000 career points.

counting on him and he possessed deep feelings for the people of the state. He was, after all, a Mountaineer at heart.

He had learned two things as a youngster growing up in the coal fields of West Virginia: the people around him valued loyalty and humility. These were, he thought, values to live by. He especially admired the ruggedness and strength of the people and resented it when they were referred to by outsiders as "a bunch of hillbillies." He saw them for what they were: honest, hardworking, and trustworthy to a fault.

"Jerry West was special to all of us," recalls Buck Harless of Gilbert, West Virginia, one of the state's wealthiest citizens and most generous philanthropists. "He never forgot where he was from and the fundamental values he learned as a youngster from Cabin Creek." At any WVU fundraising event where West appeared, the turnouts and contributions were at record highs, Harless said.

Another prominent citizen from Charleston, Russ Isaacs, called West "the ultimate icon who retained the highest degree of loyalty to the state of West Virginia. No one better typified the state and its men and women and children."

The late Ned Chilton, outspoken publisher of the *Charleston Gazette,* once told me that West was "a genuine hero, not a politician, and we needed more people like him, and fewer politicians."

Gaston Caperton, a popular two-term governor of West Virginia, laughs when he remembers that he once played in a summer basketball league game with Jerry, and they had won a game that was reported in the local newspaper. The headline read, "West and Caperton Show the Way, 30-0." All-American West scored 28 points and Caperton added two.

West proved to be everything previously advertised when he enrolled at WVU, leading the freshman team to a 17-0 season in 1956–57. As a sophomore, his first varsity year, he blossomed and scored nearly 18 points a game and averaged 11.1 rebounds. He started in all 28 games, shooting 49.6 percent from the field and 73.2 percent from the free-throw line. He was named to second-team All-American by both the Associated Press and United Press International. He was on the national map.

Mountaineer basketball loyalists, and there are many, especially remember the 1958–59 season when West led the Mountaineers to the NCAA Final Four, losing the national championship to the University of California at Berkeley by a single point, 71-70. He contributed 28 points and 11 rebounds in the loss to the Bears, and was named Most Outstanding Player in that season's Final Four.

"That loss still haunts me," West declared. "It was the first of many heartbreaks. Most importantly, I wanted that national trophy for the people of West Virginia. I wanted them to feel proud."

For the entire year, he averaged 26.6 points and 12.3 rebounds a game. He was a consensus All-American, a title that fueled universal pride in West Virginia. "His name was on everyone's lips," veteran Morgantown sportswriter Mickey Furfari remembered. "No one was bigger, ever."

Despite this enormous success, Jerry West was never satisfied with his own performance. He often brooded between games, especially when the Mountaineers came up short. "I lived it," he told me. "I was driven to do better." He remained alone in his thoughts much of the time. Some claim he did not speak to coaches for weeks at a time.

As a senior he was even better, scoring 29.3 points a game, 134 season-assists, 16.5 rebounds a game, and had a shooting average of 50.4 percent from the field and 76.6 percent from the free-throw line. He was, once again, an All-American, leaving Morgantown with 12 WVU all-time records. The university would never find another Jerry West, or so the fans believed.

The man that some called "Zeke from Cabin Creek" brought international attention to his native state and to the United States in 1960 when he co-captained the summer Olympics basketball team with Oscar Robinson. They paired to bring gold to America. "Oscar was a tremendous basketball player," West recalls. "He did so many things well and we became close friends."

And how important was West Virginia University to Jerry West? He eventually gave the university more money than he had earned from a highly successful professional basketball playing career. I could find no professional athlete who had been more generous to his alma mater. He proved his loyalty, time after time. He believed the university was central to the well being of his state and its young. He thought the state would be no greater than its flagship institution of higher learning. He still believes this.

"WVU continues to open doors for its graduates," West contends, hoping that WVU will offer ample opportunity to keep more and more gifted graduates in the state. "Education is a powerful key in life." He worries about the low number of high school and college graduates from his home state.

During his stellar 14-year career as a member of the Los Angeles Lakers, Jerry West was brilliant in all aspects of the game. He was known in the National Basketball Association for a deadly jump shot, for his tenacious defense, for his obsessive perfection, for unabashed confidence, and for a heretofore unseen will to win.

As NBA Commissioner David Stern reminded members of my class at Princeton University, West was an NBA All-Star every year of his career and led the Lakers to the NBA Finals nine times. Stern said his feats, especially under pressure, are legendary, explaining his nickname, "Mr. Clutch."

When he retired in 1974, he held records for career post season scoring and the highest average in a playoff series. Stern saw him as "perhaps the greatest guard in pro history," although he was a forward in college.

Jerry West's left-handed dribbling silhouette is used in the

NBA's official logo and he has been voted as one of the 50 greatest players in the history of the league.

Hall of Fame college and professional basketball coach Larry Brown believes that Jerry was equally effective on offense and on defense. "He was quick as a cat," Brown told me. "Jerry was something to behold. He never gave up regardless of the score."

When you repeat what others have said about him, Jerry West becomes uncomfortable and shifts the conversation to other players. For example:

"Wilt Chamberlain was many things, but always unbelievably competitive. He was often moody, complicated, and insecure. I really liked him."

"Oscar Robinson was a gifted ball handler, perhaps unrivaled. He had a unique way of blocking shots of other players at strategic times. His ability to score is well documented. Some said he was a larger version of me."

"My long-time friend and teammate Elgin Baylor had great instincts, in knowing when and how to score. He stands above the crowd, in my book. He is very special."

"Bill Russell never stopped being highly competitive. No one was a better shot blocker. He drove us wild."

"Michael Jordan's accomplishments reflect a long line of extraordinary performances. He always seemed to come through at the right time for the Bulls."

"If the game was on the line and you had one final shot, I would give the basketball to Kobe Bryant."

"LeBron James is simply the best of today's players. He has finesse while being totally intimidating. He is the entire package."

"Today's NBA players are bigger and stronger and better conditioned."

West revealed that he always battled depression as a player and it is not uncommon for others who strive for perfection in athletics to suffer from it. West believes "the great athletes

Courtesy of West Virginia University Department of Athletics

Jerry West is the pride of West Virginia.

usually pay a steep price for their success."

Jerry paid a high price physically, breaking his nose no fewer than nine times. He never worried about the way his play might impact his body. He only knew how to play one way—full speed ahead. Despite his well-documented intensity, West was one of the most admired players in the rough-and-tumble world of professional basketball. He was known for his integrity and sportsmanship.

At six-foot four inches, he played before millions of anxious people in a world of gifted giants. With Elgin Baylor ("Mr. Inside") and Jerry West ("Mr. Outside") in place, the Los Angeles Lakers became a feared opponent throughout the NBA. Only the Boston Celtics and the New York Knicks seemed to cause the Lakers sustained anguish on the hardwoods.

On July 9, 1968, the Lakers stunned the basketball world with a big-time trade, bringing the reigning NBA Most Valuable Player Award winner Wilt Chamberlain of the Philadelphia 76ers to Los Angeles at the outset of the 1968–69 basketball season. West remembers that he instantly bonded with the new addition, but Chamberlain could be difficult, often arguing with team captain Elgin Baylor and Coach Van Breda Kolff. The dressing room was filled with tension.

The coach thought Chamberlain was egotistical and that he slacked off during practice. He also thought Chamberlain was overly concerned with his own statistics.

In the 1969–70 NBA season, under a new coach, Joe Mullaney, the Lakers were dealt a crushing blow when Chamberlain suffered a serious knee injury and missed much of the regular season. West was called upon to fill the void, leading the league in scoring with an average of 31.2 points per game.

In the 1972 finals, the Lakers met the New York Knicks and ended up winning their first NBA championship. As for West, he thought he had a mediocre series and gave much of the credit for the title to Chamberlain. As an aside, Jerry had scored 4,002 playoff points, which set an all-time NBA record at the time, but he was not satisfied as a competitor.

West retired following the 1974–75 season, saying he was "not willing to sacrifice my standards." Many others thought he could have been productive for a couple more seasons, but he believed it was time and he has no regrets.

West became the Lakers coach for the 1976–77 season. He led Los Angeles for three seasons, always making the playoffs and reaching the Western Conference Finals once in 1977. He moved on to scout for the Lakers for three seasons and then he became the general manager for the 1982–83 season. On his watch, the Lakers became a power in the always-tough NBA, and the man from Cabin Creek was credited for the 1980s dynasty, which brought four championship rings to the City of Angels.

Perhaps his most famous move came in 1996 when he acquired Shaquille O'Neal via free agency and traded for shooting guard Kobe Bryant. West recruited Phil Jackson as coach. It was apparent that the foundation for continued Laker success had been skillfully laid, resulting in three more NBA titles from 2000 through 2002.

After being an integral part of the Los Angeles organization for more than 40 years, the WVU graduate retired, but he soon accepted the challenge to lead the Memphis Grizzlies as general manager in 2002. He turned the franchise into a solid playoff team, and won his second NBA Executive of the Year award in 2004. He retired a second time in 2007, this time for good.

Without question, Jerry West has shown, time after time, his belief in loyalty and humility. Often he speaks about these virtues in terms of what he has learned in West Virginia and at its state university in Morgantown. As a highly visible expression of respect, WVU has used replicas of Jerry's profile on the official Mountaineer statues in front of the Coliseum and the Student Union. No name is more revered on the campus than Jerry West. His son, Jonnie, is a member of the West Virginia Mountaineers basketball squad, and the West family maintains residences in Los Angeles and at the Greenbrier in West Virginia.

Champion Braves . . .

Ted Turner, Stan Kasten, and John Schuerholz.

One of a **kind,**
Stan Kasten

Stan Kasten is in a league of his own, being the only person in the history of professional sports to hold the position of president of three different teams at the same time. Amazing and true.

As president of the Atlanta Braves, Atlanta Hawks, and Atlanta Thrashers, he has directed a sports empire, one of enormous breadth, challenge, and complexity, and one that made a lot of money. And what did he do in his spare time? He planned and built two of America's finest sports and entertainment facilities— Turner Field for baseball and the Phillips Arena for basketball, hockey, and concerts.

Reporters, fans, and students of sports management often wonder just what it took to engineer the highly successful Hawks of the 1980s and the Braves of the 1990s, two of the giants in athletic achievement.

Among his imposing accomplishments, Kasten holds a 1995 World Series Championship, and his Braves and Hawks teams combined to make 30 playoff appearances and capture 15 division titles. When Kasten held the reins in Atlanta, the Braves won more games than any team in Major League Baseball and the team was hailed as one of the games' model franchises.

Even more impressive is the fact that the native of New Jersey was the "sports guy" for Ted Turner, the legendary rebel with uncommon vision and combativeness in the world of business. He worked with Turner for 25 years, "never experiencing a dull day."

Kasten delights in telling seldom-heard stories about Ted Turner, both because of his long-standing loyalty and respect

for the man and because many of the tales are compelling
and humorous.

Perhaps his favorite story describes a news conference at the
opening of Turner Field in 1997. Ted used the momentous occa-
sion to blast Kasten for the "high concession prices" at the new
stadium named in his honor. All Kasten could do was hold his
head and laugh. "Twenty-five years with Ted Turner," he told me.
"You never knew what was coming next."

Everyday was an uncharted experience with Turner, often
starting early in the morning and ending late at night. It was an
exciting time to be a part of the Turner team, with the company
venturing in many different directions.

Turner and his people thrived in an entrepreneurial atmo-
sphere, and he especially liked the energy of young minds,
people who were ready and able to run with a good idea, like
Stan Kasten. Turner especially admired self-starters. Those who
wanted to climb the management ladder with Turner and his
operations were expected to come up with heretofore unknown
ideas, create plans for their implementation, and run with them.

Turner empowered the individuals who worked with him in
his massive empire as they gained his trust. "Ted was the leading
attention getter and cheerleader for everything," Kasten recalls
with a smile. "He was the boss, and there was no confusion
about that."

There were quite a few "unfortunate moments" and "dangerous pitfalls." As a member of the "in-house apology team," Kasten
often joined other colleagues in wording responses to unfortunate or controversial things the boss had said. The media loved
Turner's off-the-cuff comments—the more outrageous the better.
He was a reporter's dream in the early years.

Stan Kasten fiercely defends his friend and old boss when he
insists that "Ted was never mean-spirited or malicious." He was
"having fun" with his many observations. One needs to remem-

ber that most of his verbal missteps or gaffs were made during
the early days of political correctness, and women especially
liked to use him as a public punching bag.

Turner's deep appreciation for Kasten included an invitation
to Ted's 70th birthday party, an invitation much sought after and
coveted in Atlanta.

Like countless others of his era, Kasten dreamed of having
a career in college or professional sports, not having a clue on
how to achieve that elusive and attractive end. Lightning struck
in 1976, shortly after he had graduated from Columbia Law
School and passed the bar exams for New York and New Jersey.
He decided to take a whirlwind 10-day trip around the country,
seeing baseball games and old ballparks. He was young, ambitious, and broke.

On one of the last nights of the marathon excursion, he was
in St. Louis for a game with the Cardinals and the Braves and he
spotted Ted Turner, then an obscure new Major League Baseball
owner. Kasten approached him and entered into a conversation
and offered his services. They instantly hit it off, and Turner,
clearly impressed, gave him his card and asked him to write a
letter enumerating his ideas. Weeks later, Turner invited him to
Atlanta; when he got there, Ted offered him a job beginning as a
$200-a-week legal counsel. That was the first step in what would
lead to one of the most extraordinary and storied careers in
sports history.

Kasten especially enjoys reaching out to well-prepared young
men and women who are eager to pursue a career in sports
management. He lectured to one of my classes at Princeton University several years ago and said that the profession demanded
young people who were willing to work long hours, be committed and creative, be fan-friendly, and do everything from greeting
a governor to getting coffee for the office staff. No one is treated
in a preferential way—no one—and stripes must be earned, not

given. These are the times that separate the wannabes from the eventual leaders in sports administration, Kasten believes.

"It would be impossible to get a sports job the way I did," he has explained to me. "It would be like asking a lottery winner for advice on how to win the lottery. What you have to do is gain insight and intellectual strength through studies in economics, business, management, law, and the history of sports," he suggested. "The key is to be prepared to take advantage of opportunities when they do present themselves."

Kasten had studied all the normal concerns of sports, such as contracts, antitrust, and labor, and he was current on baseball ownership and management rules and regulations. He made friends with many people who were ambitious and in the management of sports teams, believing in the importance of bonding. By doing so, he learned many lessons that would later serve him well.

The multitalented executive was asked by the students at Princeton about Ted Turner as a person and a teacher. His response seemed to surprise the class; "Ted did not spend a lot of individual time with any of us, but there was much to learn from watching him and following his lead." According to the guest lecturer, Turner had core beliefs about being bold and taking risks, and in spending money to fix a problem or start a project, especially when there was an upside payoff. "He was a firm believer in building for the upside," Kasten asserted.

In 1979, Kasten became the youngest general manager in National Basketball Association history when Turner promoted him to that position with the Hawks. He was later twice named NBA Executive of the Year.

In 1986, he moved up to the job of president of the Hawks, and eight months later took over the same duties with the Braves. Finally, in 1999, Turner tapped him to be president of Atlanta's professional hockey franchise, the Thrashers. He thrived on inordinate challenges and long hours, many of which were spent talking with fans, face to face. Kasten loved to debate with anyone.

One cannot overstate the impact that working with Ted Turner for so many years had on Kasten. He grew to see Turner as a modern-day visionary and innovator and "fearless in combat." Many contend, and I am among them, that Turner and Al Neuharth were the two most formidable media giants of the 20th century.

Both were creative in delivering the news. Turner brought unmatched skills to cable news through his network of programming, while Neuharth beat the odds by launching *USA Today,* America's largest daily newspaper.

Interestingly, Neuharth also visited a class of mine at Princeton University and said "creative risk takers like Ted Turner are the ones who fill the pages of history." They know and respect each other, though they are not friends. Virtually every cable news network has added and subtracted from the original Turner formula of operation over the years. The same can be said for Neuharth's *USA Today.*

Kasten was an original too, making close friends with nearly everyone in authority over his three sports. He was an enjoyable rogue at times, and difficult to dislike.

During my years as president of Major League Baseball's American League, I talked with Turner on a number of occasions and always found him to be entertaining and abrasive. He seemed to delight in catching one off guard with his sometimes off-the-wall, unvarnished observations, but he was always honest and impossible to misunderstand. He appeared to have few friends within baseball, and he seemed bored by the business aspects of the game.

David Stern, commissioner of the NBA, has likened Stan Kasten to a fighter who enjoys "winning the battle." Gary

Bettman, commissioner of the NHL and a long-time friend, sees him as one who "dares to be different." MLB Commissioner Bud Selig regards him as "a person of integrity who never steps back from what he thinks is right." All three commissioners who lectured to my classes at Princeton University consider Kasten a one-of-a-kind skilled operative in sports.

He is generally recognized by owners from all sports as being extremely well-versed in matters having to do with player unions, player agents, and media contracts. He holds strong views on many labor issues, and he is seen as problematic by some of the union leaders.

When Kasten agreed to take over the Braves in 1986, he spent months poring over every facet of the operation. The business model, he told Turner, simply would not produce the winner that the owner so badly wanted. At the time, the model was fueled by a desire to create attractive programming for Turner's superstation, TBS, on which the team relied for the funds to acquire expensive free agent baseball talent.

"I don't need a speech," Turner told Kasten. "Just fix it. Just fit it." And fix it he did, switching to a fundamentally different approach, investing more in player development, acquiring additional minor league teams, signing more draft picks, and improving minor league facilities. People in the game applauded Atlanta's new and seemingly realistic approach to winning, and the team of Kasten, general manager John Schuerholz, and manager Bobby Cox were its poster children.

"In baseball you really need to focus on scouting, player development, and minor leagues," Kasten contended. "All those things require time and money, and we're absolutely determined and dedicated to do it that way."

Kasten has had a magical touch when it comes to attracting large, enthusiastic crowds. During his time in Atlanta, the Braves had 13 consecutive seasons with more than two million fans in the seats, the Hawks set team attendance records in the later 1980s, and the Thrashers, an expansion team, set an average attendance record of 17,205 per game.

Not everyone likes Kasten or the way he operates; some believe he is arrogant, too quick to criticize, unduly sensitive to criticism, too glib with the ticket-buying public, and, at times, a poor listener. "I don't mean to be any of those things," he laments. "I do have a passionate, self-confident style when I am trying to make a point."

He believes he is only as good as the people around him, and they have "rarely minced words with me." He says he always strives to be a better person and welcomes opposing remarks. He has crossed blades with the media from time to time.

Of the three sports—baseball, basketball, and hockey—he believes that baseball is the most difficult to administer, remembering that each MLB organization has more than 200 players from all over the world, has to project the five-year development of high school players, and has no salary cap to keep a level playing field among the teams. What is more, Kasten notes, there is far more media and government scrutiny of baseball than the other sports because of its history as "a vital part of American history and lore."

He further believes that it is not difficult to hire great young candidates who want to be in the "glamorous business of professional sports," who offer high energy, a willingness to work long hours in a media fish bowl, and who are not too timid to be afraid of making any mistakes. "The mistakes will be there," he says. "And the successful people will learn from these and not make the same mistake twice."

Jerome Holtzman, accomplished sports columnist for the *Chicago Tribune,* once told me that Kasten was a "highly successful mentor to many young people in the sporting world," and he always regarded Kasten as one of baseball's "premier administrators."

Stan Kasten left the Turner organization in 2001 when Turner sold his sports properties. Kasten took time to read more, become more involved with his family, and volunteer for charities that held special appeal to him. Most importantly, he had time to think about what was important to him as a person and a professional.

After three years of doing other things, he decided to return to baseball, the game that most inspired him. He accepted the presidency and partial ownership of the now Washington Nationals, and once Montreal Expos, in the National League.

The move to Washington was bitterly opposed by Peter Angelos, owner of the neighboring Baltimore Orioles, but Commissioner Selig thought the sprawling area could support two major league franchises despite vastly different cultures and populations in the two cities. Major League Baseball announced in July 2006 that it had chosen the Lerner Enterprises group, led by billionaire real estate developer Theodore N. Lerner, to buy the club for $450 million.

One of Stan Kasten's first challenges was to build a state-of-the-art stadium, one that would seat 41,000 fans and offer a breathtaking view of the United States Capitol. It would be his second as a club president, an achievement of only a few. Drawing upon his well-documented years of unprecedented experience, he has positioned the Washington Nationals of the National League for a long run of success.

An *original,*
Bud Selig

Relatively few of the 78 million people who attended Major League Baseball games in 2008 know much about Bud Selig, the commissioner and the person. A few of the older fans might recall that he brought baseball back to Milwaukee after the Braves left for Atlanta, and that he owned the Brewers for many years.

Others might recognize him in a picture, especially if shown with the legendary Hank Aaron, one of his closest friends, and a few more might remember that he once ended an All-Star Game in Milwaukee with a tie because the two managers ran out of pitchers after 11 innings.

Yet he has become a featured player in the modern era of player steroid use, with emotional and often ill-informed fans blaming his office for the epidemic, which has claimed the reputations of superstars like Mark McGwire, Sammy Sosa, Barry Bonds, and Roger Clemens.

Perhaps the most devastating blow came early in 2009 when Alex Rodriguez of the New York Yankees admitted to steroid use while a member of the Texas Rangers. Many in the game had hoped that the mega standout would be the eventual all-time homerun king, erasing the memory of the former leader, surly Barry Bonds of the San Francisco Giants.

The rash of revelations has been devastating to the commissioner, who personally liked and spoke glowingly of McGwire and Sosa in the past. Selig even credited them with helping Major League Baseball regain its popularity after the cancellation of the World Series in 1994.

The Commissioner . . .

Bud Selig presents the 2008 World Series Championship
trophy to David Montgomery of the Philadelphia Phillies.

The players union, club owners, and the press have all been pillared as villains in random fashion for the drug controversy. In truth, all parties associated with the game, past and present, should have been more far more observant.

Commissioner Selig wears his feelings on his sleeve when it comes to the game he loves. "This is breaking my heart," he said after learning about the Rodriguez admission. He even admitted that he was considering reinstating Hank Aaron as baseball's homerun king in the record book. Bonds broke Aaron's record of 755 homeruns in 2007, but he has been entangled with charges that he lied to a federal grand jury.

What angers the commissioner of baseball most is that his game now has the toughest drug-testing program in professional sports. He feels too many fans and politicians fail to recognize that, and tend to side with players in any drug disputes. Players are heroes to their hometown fans, and baseball bureaucrats are not. All sports, whether they are college or professional, should have been more vigilant on the drug front and acted sooner.

Always in a resolute voice, Selig has often said that the Major League Baseball drug-testing program is clearly the strictest in professional sports. He believes it is a model program for the other sports. Specifically, it calls for steroid violators to be suspended for 50 games for the first offence, 100 games for a second, and a lifetime ban for a third.

An independent administrator runs the program. Each player is tested at least twice a year and subject to additional year-round random testing. Major League Baseball also tests for amphetamines and other stimulants and the second positive results in a 25-game suspension. All suspensions are without pay.

Baseball tests on game days, both before and after games. No more than one hour's notice is given prior to the arrival of the drug tester.

On several occasions, Commissioner Selig and players union

leader Donald Fehr have been summoned to appear before hostile congressional hearings. Some members of Congress have discovered that any criticism of baseball, fair or not, means big headlines and a choice spot on the evening news. Sometimes their rants have been outrageous, just the kind that makes for a juicy sound bite for radio and television.

The son of a successful car dealer, Selig operates on his own clock, frustrating some of his associates with a passive-aggressive style of administration. It cannot be found in a business textbook, but it works for him. He always knows about where he needs to land on matters of substance, and he is a skilled player in waiting out critics.

Significantly, Major League Baseball is judged by a different standard than professional football, basketball, and hockey. And that has been true for generations. The reasons?

Baseball is tradition, uniquely American, representing high spirits, commonly held values, and fair play. It ignites memories of youth, family, and history. Baseball is, without question, America's pastime, drawing more fans in a year than football, basketball, and hockey combined.

To countless men, women, and children, a baseball game is a precious time for family bonding, a time to eat too many hot dogs buried in mustard, a time for too many sacks of peanuts and popcorn, and a time for too much soda and beverage.

Who among us has forgotten the thrill of first seeing the magic of a manicured green playing field with loved ones? Who has not been taken with the timeless beauty of the game? Enough said; case closed.

Since the beginning of Selig's tenure in 1992, first as interim commissioner and then, in 1998, as commissioner, there have been numerous changes for the better. In full disclosure, I worked for his election as president of the American League in 1998, believing that he was committed to meaningful revenue sharing. Small market teams at the time had little or no chance to compete under the existing system.

Many in the media were critical of the Selig appointment, reasoning that he could not be truly objective on matters of importance with his fellow owners. He was, after all, a member of one of the most exclusive clubs in professional sports. Owners found comfort in knowing that the commissioner understood them and their concerns for the future of the game. Even a couple former baseball commissioners were initially apprehensive about the selection.

Selig achieved the impossible when a new system of revenue sharing was incorporated in the 2002 Collective Bargaining Agreement, one that lifted sharing among the clubs from $20 million to more than $400 million, an increase of nearly 1,900 percent. The economics of the game would never be the same. Its essential elements were continued in the 2006 agreement.

Major League Baseball Photo

Bud Selig knows the always-rugged terrain.

The players union and several large market clubs were uneasy and remained unconvinced of the need for the sweeping change.

With the eventual change, competitive balance became a reality, as eight different clubs have won the last nine World Series, and 18 different teams have reached the post season the last three years. Fans, news reporters, and owners generally hail the new excitement brought on by much better competitive balance.

In addition, Selig, an influential business and civic leader in Milwaukee, insisted on a debt service rule and a competitive balance tax. He remains ever vilgilant on all economic matters, things that might threaten the future health of the game.

The commissioner beams when explaining that the current collective agreement assures labor peace through the 2011 season, a period of 16 years, and the longest such period since the beginning of the collective bargaining process 40 years ago.

In 2006, the Collective Bargaining Agreement was successfully negotiated without a work stoppage for the second consecutive time; the first came in 2002.

During the Selig tenure, gross revenues have grown from $1.2 billion in 1992 to $6.5 billion in 2008, an increase of more than 440 percent, explaining, in no small way, the commissioner's solid standing with club owners. He is paid more than $18 million a year and "he earns every dime of it," owners contend. Furthermore, franchise values have increased dramatically under Selig. "Bud has been good for business," an owner from the West Coast told me.

Impressively, Major League Baseball has established all-time attendance records in four of the last five years. The teams drew more than 78 million fans in 2008, the second-highest total ever.

And add to that figure the record 43.2 million fans that were attracted to Minor League Baseball games in 2008. Another record is possible in 2009 because of limited entertainment options available to families caused by the faltering economy. Selig credits the 176 minor league clubs from 15 leagues with "growing the game" in many parts of the United States, believing them to be "essential."

When the 1994 World Series was cancelled and the ire of the fans was incalculable, I remember a meeting with Major League Baseball's Executive Council and its stern directive to the commissioner and the American and National League presidents to devise a recovery plan within 60 days.

The draft was ready in 30 days and it was endorsed by influential owners like John Harrington of the Boston Red Sox and Carl Pohlad of the Minnesota Twins. Even a cranky George Steinbrenner of the New York Yankees signed on.

Clearly it worked, especially with the timely assistance of Baltimore's Cal Ripken, who caught the nation's eye in 1995 when he shattered the long-standing record of Yankee great Lou Gerhig for most consecutive games played. He became the face of baseball, an attractive image to millions of Americans, reminding the fan base of the merits of the game.

Then came the riveting 1998 homerun chase between Mark McGwire of the St. Louis Cardinals and Sammy Sosa of the Chicago Cubs. The pursuit and eventual toppling of the homerun record of Roger Maris matched two likeable giants and it sold untold numbers of tickets and newspapers and made daily reports of the historic event "must see television." They were the toast of Major League Baseball, and national icons.

Much to his later regret, Commissioner Selig embraced them as friends, as he did Cal Ripken. He would never be the same. He felt violated and isolated and even now he becomes steely eyed when someone raises the names of McGwire and Sosa.

He prefers to talk about the advancement of the game in the past 18 years, pointing to:

1. The introduction of interleague play, which has turned into a solid hit with fans across the country who come out in increased numbers to see the unique match ups;

2. The three division formats in the American and National Leagues, which add to the competitiveness and appeal of the game;

3. The Wild Card and the additional round of playoffs that assure more teams a chance for championship play;

4. The limited use of instant replay on homerun calls; and
5. The return of Major League Baseball to the nation's capitol, Washington, D.C., one of America's most densely
   populated and fastest growing sports markets.

With an assist from Len Coleman, former National League
president, and me, as American League president, Selig will be
remembered for the greatest ballpark construction boom in the
history of Major League Baseball. Since 1992, new and imposing
structures have risen from the ground in Arizona, Atlanta, Baltimore, Cincinnati, Cleveland, Colorado, Detroit, Houston, Milwaukee, Philadelphia, Pittsburgh, San Francisco, San Diego, Seattle,
St. Louis, Arlington, (Texas), and Washington, D.C.

New ballparks for the New York Yankees and the New York
Mets opened in 2009, and construction is underway for a new
home for the Minnesota Twins in Minneapolis. The pursuit for
new facilities for the Florida Marlins, Tampa Bay Rays, and the
Oakland Athletics is ongoing, and Selig is optimistic.

One of the commissioner's rulings that brought hi-fives from
owners, players, and the fans was his directive to umpires to
enforce the rulebook strike zone. The umpires grumbled as they
often do, but they fell in line. Even they could not defend the
wide disparity.

Another development that did not set well with more than a
few fans, players, and so-called purists was the decision to reju-
venate the All-Star Game, long a signature event for Major League
Baseball, by awarding home field advantage to the league that
won the annual World Series classic. One can expect the players
union to reopen discussion of the matter down the road.

I believe that baseball had to do something dramatic to invig-
orate the All-Star Game; it was on life support with a dwindling
radio and television audience.

Major League Baseball took a significant step forward by

launching the MLB Network on January 1, 2009. Overnight, the network reached out to more than 50 million homes, the largest launch in cable television history. Some within the game believe the network will serve to keep and increase the fan base during challenging economic times. "Its impact will be huge," Selig has said.

In 1989, minorities held only two percent of all front office positions in baseball. With the commitment and persistence of Jerry Reinsdorf, owner of the Chicago White Sox, the commissioner has boosted the number to more than 24 percent. MLB's Diverse Business Partners program has been honored as one of the top 50 U.S. corporations for multicultural business, spending more than $300 million with minority-operated businesses.

On November 7, 2008, the commissioner of Major League Baseball addressed more than 2,000 educators from across the nation at the annual Forum of the College Board in Houston. He was there at my invitation as an advisor to President Gaston Caperton of the College Board.

Most came to hear about the upcoming baseball season and their favorite teams, but instead they were given revealing insight into the man who presides over America's national pastime. He first went to bat for the educational profession, saying there is "nothing more important than what you do … nothing.

"Education provides for greater opportunities for our children, it provides for a better future, and, especially important during these difficult times, improved education of our youth will make our country better, stronger, and more competitive in the worldwide marketplace."

He called for far greater appreciation for teaching as a profession. He committed himself to that end.

Selig turned historian when he emphasized that organized baseball was well into its second century and has long enjoyed a special social compact with the people of America. He said: "The game has been there and served as a diversion through perilous times, as it has these past months during our nation's economic uncertainty. During the Civil War, there were reports of soldiers playing the game on battlefields during respites from the fighting.

"At the beginning of World War II, President Franklin Delano Roosevelt suggested to Commissioner Kennesaw Mountain Landis that he keep baseball going to provide a measure of enjoyment for the workers on the home front. Even in the aftermath of the horrific event that took place on 9/11, baseball, particularly in New York City, served as a soothing reminder of normalcy by relaunching its season a week later and playing day in and day out.

"Baseball was there during the Civil Rights Movement. In fact, our game was ahead of it.

"I have always said that baseball is a social institution with important social responsibilities and nowhere and at no time was that more evident than at Ebbets Field in Brooklyn on April 15, 1947. That was the day that Jackie Robinson made history and broke down the game's racial barrier.

"The game of baseball was integrated before President Truman integrated the United States Army.

"Baseball was integrated nearly a decade before the Civil Rights Movement began to make an impact across America. Jackie Robinson's entry into the game was and still is baseball's proudest and most important moment."

Selig recalled that "hundreds of our players" interrupted their careers to serve in the Armed Forces, including such Hall of Fame players as Hank Greenberg, Joe DiMaggio, and Bob Feller. One, the great Ted Williams, interrupted his career twice to serve his country, first in World War II and then a few years later in the Korean War, the commissioner pointed out.

Selig paused and, with feeling, said he was driven to rid the game of baseball of all illegal drugs, drugs that threaten "the youth of our great country. Baseball players are, after all, role models for countless youngsters. Nothing will slow me."

What makes his position so rewarding, he told the educators in Houston, is the feeling of giving back to the communities that care so much about baseball and its future. He estimated that MLB has donated more than $130 million in cash and in-kind contributions to charitable and community-based initiatives and that buys "a lot of good."

He showed good-natured humor when he said, "I get lots of letters from fans on all sorts of different topics. Some offer constructive suggestions; some, as you can imagine, are not meant to be shared in polite conversation."

He closed by saying "baseball's social responsibility is my top priority as commissioner."

Allan H. "Bud" Selig is 74 years old and, despite repeated threats to retire, owners, associates, and sports reporters do not take him seriously, believing that he will not be able to retreat from an ever-growing list of pressing priorities facing the game. He is not built that way. And besides, the commissioner continues to receive unanimous votes from the owners on issues he regards as game changers. How many other CEOs can do the same with their boards?

Parting
thoughts

In the preceding pages, the reader was reminded of many things, things that hopefully altered some views about people, events, and even sports; that was my objective, remembering that:

— Jackie and **Rachel Robinson** arrived on the national scene a decade before Martin Luther King, Jr., telling the people of the United States that equity and fairness were meant for men and women regardless of the color of their skin. They jointly faced hostility and threats, not having the benefit of a President John F. Kennedy or an Attorney General Robert Kennedy. They often felt alone in their unshakable beliefs that ultimately prevailed on and off the baseball field. They knew the lasting value of the ring.

— So did colorful **Bill Veeck,** who showed the sports world how to win while having fun. He spent his life reaching out to the young and the unfortunate, once enduring a 50-mile civil rights march on a wooden leg. He introduced the concept of promotions for the young and old, providing new and different entertainment on and off the diamond in Cleveland and Chicago, where he won American League championships. His antics were also popular in St. Louis, where he owned the Browns, and with minor league crowds. As the owner of the Indians, he hired the first African American, Larry Doby, to play in the American League.

— Since joining NBC Sports in the early 1980s, **Bob Costas** has reflected intelligence, thorough preparation, stunning articulation skills, unique insight, professional polish, and a touch of irreverence and wit. Media critics say he introduced a new dimension to sports broadcasting, winning an unprecedented 19 Emmy Awards. He has become the face of the Olympics for NBC, a show of athletic talent from across the globe. Costas understands and respects those men and women who have claimed the ring. Off camera, he is interested in popular culture and is always in touch with the times.

— **Gene Autry** did more than bring American League baseball to the state of California in the form of the Angels. Known to generations as the Singing Cowboy on records and in movies and television, he established a record of giving to the needy and to worthwhile societal programs. He gave because it was the right thing to do. At the time of his death, he had given more than $250 million, virtually without public attention. His record of giving surpassed that of entertainer Paul Newman, who has received universal and deserved kudos for his generosity. Autry won the ring through many years of service and countless good deeds.

— Looking somewhat menacing, as advertised, **Bob Gibson** seldom smiled even at University of Nebraska football games in Lincoln, where he did not feel the pressure to win. As an on-field assistant to me as American League president, he never minced words; he saw things as being right or wrong, and seldom in between. One of his best friends, former New York Yankees manager Joe Torre, told me that, "When necessary, Gibson had three pitches … fast, faster, and fastest. The last one was not seen." Bob Gibson was perhaps the greatest right-handed pitcher in National League history, and he knew it. He won 251 games, posted an eye-popping 2.91 earned run average, and struck out 3,117 batters for the St. Louis Cardinals during a 16-year career. Torre, now manager of the Los Angeles Dodgers, said he would not describe his friend from Omaha as unfriendly when he pitched. "Hateful was more like it," he said.

— Living in the Bay Area that has produced some of the

sporting world's greatest names, **Billy Beane,** general manager of the Oakland Athletics, is arguably the most recognizable sports figure today. Over the past decade, he has produced consistent winners with bare-bones budgets, sometimes near the bottom of Major League Baseball. His unique approach to winning became public with the publication of the bestseller *Moneyball,* by Michael Lewis, in 2003. Beane employs new statistical methods in running the A's, defying many of the approaches that old-baseball people use. A native Californian, he sometimes comes to work his shorts and sandals, always appearing at ease. He is without pretension.

— **Jerry West** started playing basketball as a kid in a small town in southern West Virginia. His court in those days was a dirt-covered clearing in a neighbor's backyard, where he spent countess hours shooting at a basketball hoop nailed to a storage shack. He went on to be an All-State high school standout and later an All-American at West Virginia University. As a professional with the Los Angeles Lakers, he was an All-Star during his entire 14-year playing career and he was third in NBA history to score 25,000 points, joining Wilt Chamberlain and Oscar Robertson. He remained loyal to his alma mater and his state, and humble to his fans.

— **Stan Kasten** was Ted Turner's "sports guy" for 25 years, and he told me "you never knew what was coming next." Kasten always lived, however, to face another day with the flamboyant entrepreneur. To be more precise, Kasten became the first person to hold the position of president of three big sports teams simultaneously—the Atlanta Braves, Atlanta Hawks, and Atlanta Thrashers. He is best known for his visable accomplishments with the Braves, winning the 1995 World Series championship and winning more games than any other team in Major League Baseball during his remarkable tenure. "Ted was fun and hard driving all at the same time," his protégé related. "He had no time for people who were without innovative suggestions."

— **Bud Selig** makes a lot of money being commissioner of Major League Baseball—well over $18 million dollars a year. And yet, he is a frequent target of fans, media, and members of Congress, who blame him for what they see as being wrong with our national pastime. He has been singled out for the alarming use of enhancing drugs by players, the manner in which Barry Bonds was handled during the all-time homerun chase, the escalating salaries of players and the resulting prices for attending baseball games, the cancellation of a World Series, and some old timers still resent that he was once an owner. His achievements are impressive, and merit objective consideration. MLB has set all-time attendance records in four of the past five years, drawing more than 78 million fans last year. Gross revenues have grown from $1.2 billion in 1992 to more than $6.5 billion in 2008, an increase of more than 440 percent. He brought labor peace to the game and real revenue sharing. In 1992, only $20 million was shared amongst the clubs and today it exceeds $400 million, an increase of nearly 1,900 percent. His revenue sharing success has heightened competitive balance among the 30 teams. Eight different clubs have won the last nine World Series trophies, and 18 different teams have reached post-season play in the last three years. Owners credit him with taking the game back from the union and they resent the continual pounding that he takes from "knee jerk critics." Without question, he loves the game and the richness of its history. I offer a prediction: Bud Selig will stay as long as he wants as commissioner; he still gets unanimous votes of approval from the owners on anything that he believes is important.

Clearly, these nine strong-willed people, like those in the previous volume, understood the value of the ring and what its acquisition might mean to them and, more importantly, to their effectiveness as leaders in varied and important areas. There is much to learn from these strikingly unique individuals.

The ring was a powerful objective in their lives, one they hoped would bring peace of mind to them and lasting joy to their families, friends, and communities. They wanted to achieve long-term credibility as individuals and meaningful gains for those who would follow them in the profession. It would, they thought, open doors of opportunity for others, men and women who would follow and learn from their strengths and weaknesses.

It was the ultimate in their collective eye, the big leagues of life, though they never talked about it in those words.

Their paths to the top of the mountain often appeared insurmountable, brimming with thorny obstacles, challenges, and great personal peril, but they never lost sight of the true objective, the end game.

Without question, this team of nine exceptional players had energized and focused intellect and the physical tools to persevere and advance in often-hostile environments. They all refused to accept defeat, or to mention the word.

They often changed directions, strategies, and game plans, but never lost the will to excel at the highest level. They learned to take punches. Many of the people around them criticized and thought them to be unrealistic dreamers. Some even laughed in a disparaging way at their efforts.

On the way to the circle of winners, all of them experienced setbacks; some so painful they refused to talk about them. Some were physical, some were personal, and some were financial, but most other people would have found these obstacles to be game ending or perhaps even terminal. Some seemed to thrive on extreme difficulty and even pain.

Despite views to the contrary, these unique and hardened individuals were poised and persistent, waiting for the right moments to leave their imprints. Each dared to lead at difficult times, while most others were willing to watch and follow.

All of them were influenced by their parents and never forgot their origins. As they have grown older, they often refer to the ways of family and to their roots. They find it reassuring and refreshing to visit their hometowns and their old school friends with growing regularity. Without question, they are proud survivors who see the value of what they have achieved and they are increasingly generous with their resources.

Of course they all would do some things differently today. They would be better organized, for one, and most said they would have somewhat longer fuses. By their own admission, they were young and impatient to move forward.

Each of them wishes that far greater attention had been given to opening gates of opportunity for deserving people of color. The importance of Jackie Robinson cannot be overstated, they say. The slowness on the affirmative action front stunted America's growth and opportunities, they believe, and they especially applaud the gains of women in the past two decades.

All are self-proclaimed patriots, believing in the might and potential of the United States of America. They all have imposing records of helping with the advancements of elementary, secondary, and higher education. They are among the country's most generous givers.

Professional sports organizations in America have been, for example, among the earliest and strongest supporters of classroom teachers. They favor needed educational reform and improvement in the classroom as ways for the young to better compete on the international scene. The same can be said of our chosen teammates from other areas, such as media, government, and politics.

All of the nine have endorsed the need for greater research in the health sciences and each has spoken through personal contributions.

All believe that the country cannot live in isolation, explaining the determination of professional sports to spread its wings globally. Furthermore, virtually all of the most important pieces of national legislation have an international aspect to them, as they should.

What is certain: Our magical nine, despite some shortcomings, will leave a legacy of huge shoes to fill in the years ahead. The ring, it would seem, is the least we can award them.

Most of them remain contrarians, but they have admittedly mellowed in open and positive ways. They especially enjoy exchanging ideas with bright youngsters, and they want to continue to give to the common good and to their chosen professional fields. They remain involved in causes, often ones they initiated and nurtured over the years. They give in ways that encourage others, especially those with substantial means. "When you give to your favorite charity or cause you revitalize yourself," Jerry West told me. He has given freely to West Virginia University, more than a million dollars.

Without question, the competitive spirit they have engendered for generations has helped to make the nation great, and that spirit is alive and well among many of our young today. Unfortunately, we have too few role models in our society like those people showcased here.

It was revealing to discover how little substantive difference there was between the first nine individuals cited and the second nine in terms of expressed values, beliefs, and determination. Each is very different, very thoughtful, and very resolute, and each is an unabashed optimist.

I offer sincere gratitude to George M. Steinbrenner, Larry Doby, Tom Osborne, Roy Williams, Gale Sayers, Jerry Reinsdorf, Bob Kerrey, Al Neuharth, and Bob Dole.

And I offer thanks to Rachel Robinson, Bill Veeck, Bob Costas, Gene Autry, Bob Gibson, Billy Beane, Jerry West, Stan Kasten, and Bud Selig.

None of the above sought entry into the two books and all agreed to participate only after being persuaded that they had something special to offer. All of them have grasped the ring, hoping to serve as a model for those who will follow. Fortunately, there is no shortage of men and women with exceptional promise in the United States.

Dr. Budig at his place of choice.

About the
author

A recognized academic leader and writer, Gene A. Budig is the distinguished professor and senior presidential advisor at the College Board in New York City. As the head of three major state universities, Illinois State University, West Virginia University, and the University of Kansas, he was responsible for the educational programs of 520,000 students. The University of Nebraska graduate served as president of Major League Baseball's American League (1994–2000) and oversaw a period of historic growth in attendance and physical facilities. He is a co-owner of the Charleston RiverDogs, the Class A entry of the New York Yankees in the South Atlantic League.

READINGS

Babcock, Mike. *Heart of a Husker, Tom Osborne's Nebraska Legacy.* Champaign, IL: Sports Publishing L.L.C., 2006.

Budig, Gene A. *A Game of Uncommon Skill.* Westport, CT: Oryx Press, 2002.

Budig, Gene A. *The Inside Pitch ... And More.* Morgantown, WV: West Virginia University Press, 2004.

Budig, Gene A. *Grasping the Ring.* Lincoln, NE: University of Nebraska Press, 2009.

Costas, Bob. *Fair Ball, A Fan's Case for Baseball.* New York: Broadway Books, 2000.

Danielson, Michael N. *Home Team: Professional Sports and the American Metropolis.* Princeton, NJ: Princeton University Press, 1997.

Dole, Bob. *One Soldier's Story.* New York: HarperCollins, 2005.

Drury, James. *The Leadership Vacuum in Professional Sports.* Chicago: Spencer Stuart, 2000.

Fort, Rodney. *Sports Economics.* New York: Prentice Hall, 2002.

Gibson, Bob, with Lonnie Wheeler. *Stranger to the Game, The Autobiography of Bob Gibson.* New York: Penguin Books, 1994.

George-Warren, Holly. *Public Cowboy No. 1. The Life and Times of Gene Autry.* New York: Oxford University Press, 2007.

Gorman, Jerry, and Kirk Calhoun. *The Name of the Game, the Business of Sports.* New York: John Wiley & Sons, Inc., 1994.

Halberstam, David. *The Breaks of the Game.* New York: Alfred A. Knopf, 1981.

Helyar, John. *Lords of the Realm.* New York: Random House, 1994.

Kahn, Roger. *October Men.* New York: Harcourt, 2003.

Kern, William, editor. *The Economics of Sports.* Kalamazoo, MI: W.E. Upjohn Institute for Employment Research, 2000.

Krantz, Les. *Reel Baseball, Baseball's Golden Era, the Way America Witnessed It.* New York: Doubleday, 2006.

Kuhn, Bowie. *Hardball.* New York: Times Books, 1987.

Levin, Richard. *The Report of the Independent Members of the Commissioner's Ribbon Panel on Baseball Economics,* July 2000.

Lomax, Michael E. *Black Baseball Entrepreneurs, 1860-1901,* Syracuse, NY: Syracuse University Press, 2003.

Lucas, Adam. *Going Home Again.* Guilford, CT: Lyons Press, 2004.

Kerrey, Bob. *When I Was a Young Man.* New York: Harcourt, 2002.

Madden, Bill. *Damned Yankees: A No-Holds-Barred Account of Life with "Boss Steinbrenner."* New York: Warner Books, 1990.

MacPhail, Lee. *My 9 Innings*. Westport, CT: Meckler Books, 1989.

Miller, Marvin. *A Whole Different Ballgame: The Inside Story of Baseball's New Deal*. New York: Simon and Schuster, 1991.

Neuharth, Al. *Confessions of an S.O.B.* New York; Doubleday, 1989.

Noll, Roger, and Andrew Zimbalist. *Sports, Jobs and Taxes: The Economic Impact of Sports Teams and Stadiums.* Washington, D.C.: Brookings Institution Press, 1997.

Olney, Buster. *The Last Night of the Yankee Dynasty.* New York: HarperCollins, 2004.

Osborne, Tom. *What It Means to Be a Husker.* Chicago: Triumph Books, 2004.

Prichard, Peter. *The Making of McPaper: The Inside Story of USA TODAY.* New York: Universal Press Syndicate, 1987.

Quirk, James, and Rodney Fort. *Pay Dirt: The Business of Professional Team Sports.* Princeton, NJ: Princeton University Press, 1992.

Quirk, James, and Rodney Fort. *Hard Ball: The Abuse of Power in Pro Team Sports.* Princeton, NJ: Princeton University Press, 1999.

Rampersad, Arnold. *Jackie Robinson, A Biography.* New York: Alfred A. Knopf, 1997.

Ritter, Lawrence S. *Lost Ballparks.* New York: Viking Penguin, 1992.

Sayers, Gale. *My Life and Times.* Chicago: Triumph Books, 2007.

Sayers, Gale, with Al Silverman. *I Am Third.* New York: The Viking Press, 1970.

Scully, Gerald. *The Business of Major League Baseball.* Chicago: University of Chicago Press, 1989.

Seymour, Harold. *Baseball: The Golden Age.* New York: Oxford University Press, 1971.

Staudohar, Paul. *The Sports Industry and Collective Bargaining.* Ithaca, NY: ILR Press, 1989.

Staudohar, Paul. *Playing for Dollars: Labor Relations and the Sports Business.* Ithaca, NY: ILP Press, 1996.

Tygiel, Jules. *Baseball's Greatest Experiment.* New York: Oxford University Press, 1984.

Veeck, Bill, and Ed Linn. *Veeck as in Wreck.* Chicago: University of Chicago Press, 1962.

Veeck, Mike, and Pete Williams. *Fun Is Good.* New York: Rodale Press, 2005.

Vincent, Fay. *The Last Commissioner.* New York: Simon and Schuster, 2002.

Whitford, David. *Playing Hardball.* New York: Doubleday, 1993.

Zimbalist, Andrew. *Baseball and Billions: A Probing Look Inside the Business of Our National Pastime.* New York: Basic Books, 1994.

Zimbalist, Andrew. *Unpaid Professionals.* Princeton, NJ:
    Princeton University Press, 1999.

Zimbalist, Andrew. *May the Best Team Win: Baseball
    Economics and Public Policy.* Washington, D.C.: Brookings
    Institution Press, 2003.